LARCENY
IN MY
BLOOD

LARCENY
IN MY
BLOOD

A Memoir of Heroin, Handcuffs, and Higher Education

Matthew Parker

GOTHAM BOOKS

GOTHAM BOOKS
Published by Penguin Group (USA) Inc.
375 Hudson Street, New York, New York 10014, U.S.A.
Penguin Group (Canada), 90 Eglinton Avenue East, Suite 700, Toronto, Ontario M4P
2Y3, Canada (a division of Pearson Penguin Canada Inc.); Penguin Books Ltd, 80 Strand,
London WC2R ORL, England; Penguin Ireland, 25 St Stephen's Green, Dublin 2, Ireland
(a division of Penguin Books Ltd); Penguin Group (Australia), 250 Camberwell Road,
Camberwell, Victoria 3124, Australia (a division of Pearson Australia Group Pty Ltd);
Penguin Books India Pvt Ltd, 11 Community Centre, Panchsheel Park, New Delhi – 110 017,
India; Penguin Group (NZ), 67 Apollo Drive, Rosedale, Auckland 0632, New Zealand
(a division of Pearson New Zealand Ltd); Penguin Books (South Africa) (Pty) Ltd,
24 Sturdee Avenue, Rosebank, Johannesburg 2196, South Africa

Penguin Books Ltd, Registered Offices: 80 Strand, London WC2R ORL, England

Published by Gotham Books, a member of Penguin Group (USA) Inc.

First printing, August 2012
10 9 8 7 6 5 4 3 2 1

LIBRARY OF CONGRESS CATALOGING-IN-PUBLICATION DATA
Parker, Matthew, 1960-
  Larceny in my blood : a memoir of heroin, handcuffs, and higher education / Matthew
Parker.
     p. cm.
  ISBN 978-1-59240-662-3
  1. Parker, Matthew, 1960—Comic books, strips, etc. 2. Ex-convicts—United States—
Biography—Comic books, strips, etc. 3. Ex-drug addicts—United States—Biography—
Comic books, strips, etc. 4. Adult college students—United States—Biography—Comic
books, strips, etc. I. Title.
  HV9468.P366A3 2012
  364.8092—dc23
  [B]
                          2011052069

Printed in the United States of America

Disclaimer: The following is a work of memory, and what is more, a memory often clouded not only by the passage of time, but so too by the fog of drug and alcohol abuse, both of which I indulged in freely for the better part of my life. I cannot thus claim complete accuracy on dialog or even some of the actual events that are covered in the memoir. It must also be noted that some of the characters' names have been changed due to privacy concerns.

Portions of this memoir were first published in *Lux*, Vol. 2, copyright © 2006, under the title "In the Spoon by Noon."

For my brothers, both of whom, in one form or another, gave up.

And for my mom and sister, who never could.

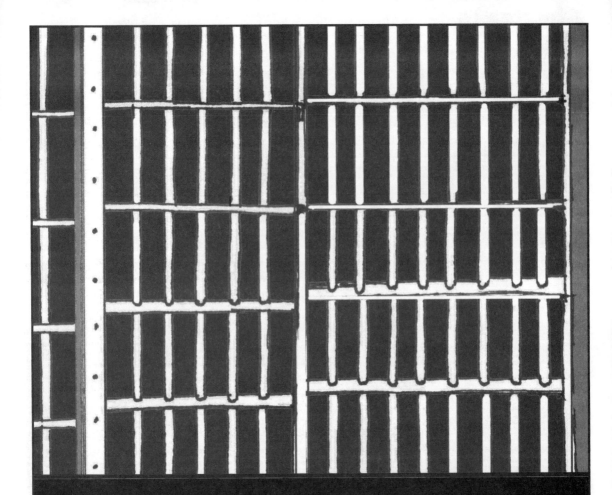

"Once, in his cell, I caught him painting cornfields in crepuscular light..."

From "Waltz with sticks," by Genevieve Burger-Weiser.

Chapter 1

I get out of prison—for the last time—on March 19, 2002, and my plan is to go to college and get a degree.

Fort Grant

No Weapons Allowed

All Vehicles Subject to Search

I visit Scottsdale Community College in Arizona to apply for financial aid.

All Vehicles Subject to Tickets

Their mascot is the Fighting Artichoke.

SCC

In 1972, the administrators decided to funnel money away from academics and into athletics, which pissed off the student government.

More money for scholarships for out-of-state athletes.

And a new gym.

No. We need financial aid for the poor and disadvataged, like the Pima Indians.

Scottsdale Community College, or SCC, was built on the Salt River Pima-Maricopa Indian Community.

Better known as "the reservation."

In 1973, the student government voted to spend more money on scholarships and to build a daycare center for students with children, but the powers that be vetoed both proposals and censored the student newspaper.

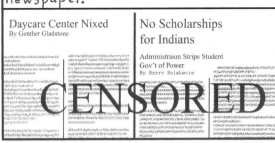

Most of the money went to build the gym and recruit jocks from out of state. The administration stripped the student government of all power, save the choosing of the team mascot.

TEXAS   UTAH

The result of which really pissed off the administrators...

A what?

...not to mention the jocks.

A fucking artichoke.

His name's Artie.

A soft, squishy, faggoty fucking artichoke.

SCC

10

There were no artichokes in prison.

If there were, I would have had to pretend that I hated their green skin.

Just like I had to pretend I hated black skin, or brown, or yellow, or indeed anyone who was not a so-called "Aryan."

Hate so thick and regimented that I wasn't even allowed to watch the most popular TV show of the 1990s.

No Jews for you.

2

Once in the financial aid office, I panic over the question: "Have you ever been convicted of possession or sales of narcotic drugs?"

Oh fuck!

I was sent to prison three times for possession.

October 1990						
	1	2	3	4	5	6
7	8	9	10	11	12	13
14	15	16	17	18	19	20
21	22	23	24	25	26	27
28	27	28	29	30	31	

April 1992						
			1	2	3	4
5	6	7	8	9	10	11
12	13	14	15	16	17	18
19	20	21	22	23	24	25
26	27	28	29	30	31	

May 1995						
	1	2	3	4	5	6
7	8	9	10	11	12	13

But I was never sent to prison for, say, kidnapping Rush Limbaugh.

Hey there, fat boy.

Hello.

Even if I did have a prior conviction for kidnapping Rush Limbaugh, it wouldn't have prevented me from receiving financial aid.

I thought we should meet, one junkie to another.

How do you do?

Only a possession or sales charge can do that.

I'm fine. You?

Sure you can. Just as soon as you crawl through the eye of this needle.

Ok, I guess. Can I leave now?

No Problem.

I'm approved for financial aid because I have been "satisfactorily rehabilitated," whatever that means.

FAFSA
Free Application for Federal Student Aid

APPROVED

Just so long as I don't get another possession charge; that would stop my financial aid immediately.

You're under arrest for possession of heroin. I hope you realize this totally fucks your financial aid.

In the halls of institutional education, the penalties for kidnapping are much less severe than getting busted with a few joints.

Suppose I held someone captive for a week?

Not a problem. It's liberal narcotics that interest us.

Office of Financial Aid

But I decide to pass on the kidnapping for now, and get a job to hold me over until school starts in the fall.

Don't care how many felonies ya got. The pay is $5.20 an hour and this here's the only tool you'll ever need.

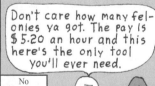

No Smoking, Drinking, Spitting, Sleeping, Loitering,

No Boots No Work No Exceptions

All Tools Must Be Turned in to Get Your Pay

I have a number of trades under my belt.

RESUME

Carpenter
Drywaller
Roofer
Electrician
Tile setter
Machinist
Mechanic

Mostly in construction.

I'm the proverbial "Jack of all trades, master of none."

The problem is I have no truck and a suspended and revoked driver's license and, for the first time in 20 years, I refuse to drive without one.

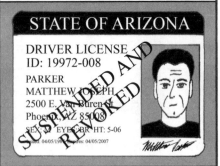

STATE OF ARIZONA

DRIVER LICENSE
ID: 19972-008
PARKER
MATTHEW JOSEPH
2500 E. Van Buren St.
Phoenix, AZ 85008
SEX: M EYES: BR HT: 5-06
Issued: 04/05/198 Expires: 04/05/2007

SUSPENDED AND REVOKED

I owe thousands of dollars in unpaid civil tickets for speeding and driving without insurance. I also have a number of criminal tickets like driving on a suspended license. I have overdue fines in courts all over the Phoenix metro area. To make matters worse, Phoenix mass transit sucks.

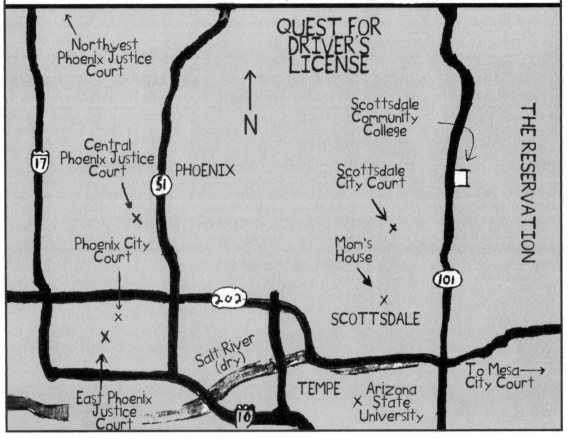

QUEST FOR DRIVER'S LICENSE

N

Northwest Phoenix Justice Court

Scottsdale Community College

17

Central Phoenix Justice Court

51 PHOENIX

Scottsdale City Court
X

Phoenix City Court

Mom's House
X

202

SCOTTSDALE

THE RESERVATION

101

X

X

Salt River (dry)

To Mesa City Court

East Phoenix Justice Court

TEMPE

Arizona State University
X

10

4

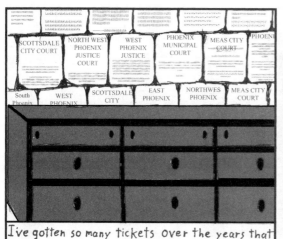

I've gotten so many tickets over the years that I could use them for wallpaper.

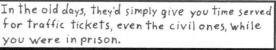

In the old days, they'd simply give you time served for traffic tickets, even the civil ones, while you were in prison.

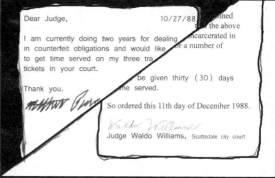

Dear Judge,   10/27/88

I am currently doing two years for dealing in counterfeit obligations and would like to get time served on my three traffic tickets in your court.

Thank you.

...be given thirty (30) days time served.

So ordered this 11th day of December 1988.

Judge Waldo Williams, Scottsdale city court

All you had to do was write to each court.

The criminal tickets had to be taken care of before your release.

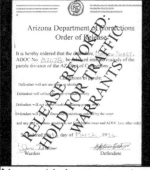

Arizona Department of Corrections
Order of Release

You couldn't get out of prison with active warrants.

I spent a good deal of my years in federal and Arizona State prisons writing judges to get time served on my traffic tickets.

On my last sentence, however, none of the courts will honor my request.

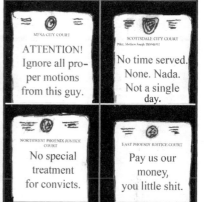

MESA CITY COURT
ATTENTION! Ignore all proper motions from this guy.

SCOTTSDALE CITY COURT
No time served. None. Nada. Not a single day.

NORTHWEST PHOENIX JUSTICE COURT
No special treatment for convicts.

EAST PHOENIX JUSTICE COURT
Pay us our money, you little shit.

I was released from Fort Grant with warrants out for my arrest because each court wanted their money.

Here's your 50 bucks. You can use it as a down payment on all those tickets.

ASPC-SAFFORD FORT GRANT

NO WEAPONS BEYOND THIS POINT

R&D ALL PRISONERS MUST BE CUFFED
NO EXCEPTIONS
AZ DEPT OF CORRECTIONS

This is new to me, and the main reason I can't legally drive.

Arizona Department of Motor Vehicle

I would like to get my license reinstated, please.

Ho, ho, ho

Hee, hee, hee,

Ha, ha, ha,

NOW SERVING NUMBER
B-76

I also owe about $8,000 in fines for my felonies. Arizona uses these unpaid fines to withhold my voting rights.

STATE OF ARIZONA
VOTER REGISTRATION

FELONS MUST HAVE PAID ALL THEIR FUCKING FINE MONEY TO BE ELIGIBLE.

The rule is simple: Can't pay, can't vote.

Arizona also legally bars felons from renting apartments.

APTS. FOR RENT
1 & 2 Bedroom Units
Starting at $800
NO PETS OR EX CONS ALLOWED

So called "crime-free zones" which are, at last count, just about everywhere.

It's not surprising that this was a very popular tattoo on Arizona state prison yards.

Luckily I had a place to go upon my release: my mom's house in Scottsdale.

Every time I went to prison, my fifth trip this time, Mom was always there for me when I got out.

If you stay clean, I'll buy you a Harley.

"Being there for me" is easier said than done. I've been a junkie for 20-plus years, despite the best efforts of my mom and others.

I fix a week after my release, although I convince anyone who'll listen that I didn't.

I'm not high.

I'm checking my eyelids for pinholes.

Except Mom. There's no fooling Mom. She'd seen me high too many times to be fooled by me now.

Are you high?

You fucking liar.

Wha...? No.

In my third week after being released from Prison, I shoot too much heroin.

The most dangerous time for junkies is when they're completely clean; the chance of an overdose increases substantially when they shoot up an amount they used to be able to handle.

RIP
JUST ONE
MORE
DEAD
JUNKIE

I crawl into the shower and blast the cold water on my naked body in an effort to bring myself out of it.

My mom finds me there, groggy but still alive.

What the fuck?

I'm sorry.

She's in complete despair.

She can see the future. I'll be strung out within a month...

...and be back in jail or prison within a year.

The level of sad acceptance on my mom's face motivates me to stay clean. I vow that it's the last time I'll ever stick a needle in my arm.

But it ain't easy.

No sex no drugs no women no speedballs no car no Harley no cell Phone no hookers...

no fake fuck-ing tits even to suck on so why in the fuck shouldn't I get high?

I use once or twice after that, but the magic is gone, I decide, once and for all, to never use again.

In the fifties my mom eloped with my dad on his Harley.

"Faster faster."

Route 66

They got married in Manassas, Virginia.

She was 25 in 1960, the year I was born.

Amphetamines   Barbiturates

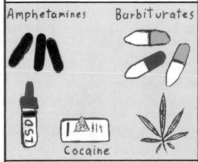

LSD   Cocaine

Ten years later, she was familiar with all the drugs of that generation. Although she experimented, Pot was the only drug she took to.

In the seventies, Mom was flying Mexican marijuana on commercial flights from Phoenix to New York.

Mom

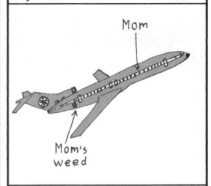

Mom's weed

We would then sell it in Connecticut.

My mom and dad had four kids. We were all born in Bridgeport, Connecticut, an industrial city on Long Island Sound, 60 miles east of Manhattan.

Mark (1961)   Me (1960)   John (1957)   Denise (1956)

We were not your average American family.

My father was not only a drunk but was physically and mentally abusive— to all of us, but to my mom most of all.

"You no-good fucking whore. Where have you been? Who were you with? I know Matthew ain't my kid."

In retaliation, she stopped cooking for him, bleached her hair blonde, and began swearing like a sailor.

"No dinner again?"

"Cook it yourself you fucking dick."

Eventually he got fed up and just moved out. None of us was sorry to see him go. They divorced in 1965.

GET THE HELL OUT! DO IT YOURSELF RENTALS "We Endeavor to Understand"

She took a low-paying job and almost immediately turned to larceny, mostly with crimes like shoplifting.

EYE of The Round $1.99 LB.

BUTT CH K $

She then collected welfare while working. A serious felony, Mom was evolving criminally...

...and she moved up to smuggling in 1972.

Mom was paying $75 a pound in Arizona. She sold it for $150 a pound to dealers while I sold it by the ounce. I made twenty grand my first year, when I was 13.

Ten pounds—that's $1,500.

One ounce—that's 20 bucks.

Of course we boys all started getting high at a very young age. In our early teens. Nor was it just on that crappy green weed mom was smuggling.

I was 16 the first time I stuck a needle in my arm.

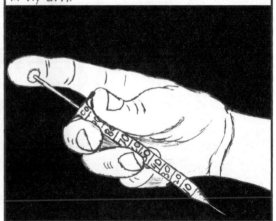

The only person in my family ever to do so.

The worst I ever did was huff glue.

I smoked PCP a few times.

I got drunk once.

John preferred barbiturates and alcohol.

Mark, after his initial, experimental phase, didn't like drugs at all.

And Denise substituted education for drugs.

This despite the fact that it was the mid-seventies, and everyone else was getting high. Even the square kids who weren't allowed to hang out with me. I knew this because I sometimes had to sell to them.

We need a lid, man. We wanna get baked and listen to kiss.

Yeah, kiss.

John and I used to sell fake acid at Kiss concerts.

Four-way windowpane.

Get your blotter acid.

PALACE

But geeks are not limited to kiss fans or eggheads in physics labs.

$$G_{\mu\nu} + \Lambda \hat{g}_{\mu\nu} = \frac{8\pi G}{c^4} T_{\mu\nu}$$

$$G_{\mu\nu} + \Lambda g_{\mu\nu} = \frac{8\pi G}{c^4} T_{\mu\nu}$$

$$H^2 = \left(\frac{\dot{a}}{a}\right)^2 = \frac{8\pi G}{3}\rho - \frac{kc^2}{a^2} + \frac{\Lambda c^2}{3}$$

Prisons and jails are full of them. Especially the jails.

After I shot the clerk...

...I hid the money in my car.

Jailhouse Snitch

We called them "LOPs," for L.O.P., or Loss of Privileges.

Disciplinary Report Form

Inmate: Gunther Gladstone #1999999
Violation(s): 33B - Tattooing, and 01C - Altering of physical appearance: Inmate Gladstone has a new tattoo (devil's horns) on his forehead

Recommended sanction: 30 days LOP

Arizona Department of Corrections

"L.O.P." is given to inmates for minor, stupid, and usually laughable write-ups. "Lop" is a prison word for a geek.

This is a birds-eye view of a typical Maricopa County Jail housing unit.

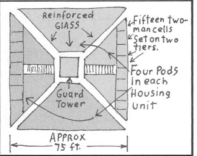

Reinforced GLASS

Fifteen two-man cells set on two tiers.

Four Pods in each Housing Unit

Guard Tower

APPROX 75 ft.

There are sixteen such housing units in the six-story, Madison Street Jail, located in downtown Phoenix.

The county jail is where you are held after your arrest. It is basically a holding facility for guys going to court. It is close, crowded, and confining to the extreme. The food is bad. Jails are designed with discomfort in mind so you will sign that plea bargain quick!

And this is a prison. The medium security, Federal Correctional Institute just north of Phoenix. Unlike a county jail, it's spread out, less confining. General population prisoners are housed in three units: Pima, Navajo, and Mohave. Yuma is reception and Mesa is a snitch unit. FCI-Phoenix houses sentenced prisoners, most of whom work during the day and enjoy a few hours of free time each evening.

Average sentence: fifteen years. With just a two-year sentence, I was doing wino time and was often razzed about it. Still, it was a federal prison—a few steps up from a state prison, and miles above a fucking county jail.

There were perhaps 700 men on the main yard when I was there in the late 1980s. Although blessed with much more freedom (and better food) than county jail, I was still locked up. The double fences brimmed with razor wire, guards patrolled the fence line in pickup trucks, and helicopter wires (designed to keep helicopters from landing) were strung thirty or so feet above the entire complex to prevent airborne escapes.

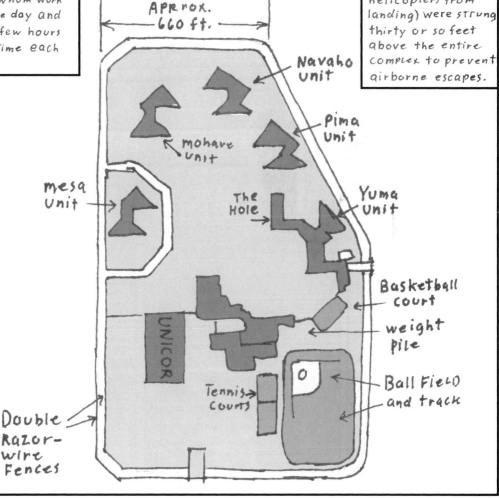

APPROX. 660 ft.

Navaho Unit

Pima Unit

Mohave Unit

mesa Unit

The Hole

Yuma Unit

Basketball court

weight pile

UNICOR

Tennis Courts

Ball Field and track

Double Razor-wire Fences

My dream was always to attend the fed joints of higher learning, the Ivy League.

BROWN
COLUMBIA
CORNELL
DARTMOUTH
HARVARD
PENN
PRINCETON
YALE

When we were kids, my mom always talked up fed joints...

The trick is not to go to prison at all...

...but if you do have to go, go federal.

...not to mention college.

A college degree from a good law school will put you in a position of legalized larceny.

As an adolescent, I'd always wanted to attend Columbia.

THE NEW YORK CRIMES
COLUMBIA RIOTS OF 1968—FIVE YEARS LATER
PALESTINE U.S. INVOL.

But I got too caught up in crime and drugs.

A nickel bag of weed equals two hits of LSD.

Being poor was a conditioned response in my family, to the point where stealing became second nature.

Why'd you steal that candy bar when you make a small fortune selling pot?

It's in my blood.

Guilt only manifested if you couldn't steal.

Why didn't you steal that candy bar?

I was scared.

You fucking pussy.

That's what my family says.

By 1977, I'd already been arrested three times.

Bridgeport Police Department
State of Connecticut

Arrest record: Matthew Parker
DOB: 4/5/1960

6/7/76   Criminal Mischief

8/22/76   Reckless Driving,
         Evasion of Responsibility

10/27/77   Larceny (four)

My brother John even more.

Third time this month for this one.

What's the charge?

Auto theft.

But when Mark got busted for burglary and gun charges, the extra heat shut down the pot business...

Stealing firearms?

You're in serious trouble, young man.

...and everything changed.

We got lids for sale, man.

Yeah, lids.

After some stern warnings from local police, we did what any good criminal family would do.

We ran. My mom and her boyfriend, Carl, along with Mark and I (John and Denise stayed behind), moved from Bridgeport, Connecticut, to the deep woods of Coal City, Pennsylvania, in the autumn of 1977...

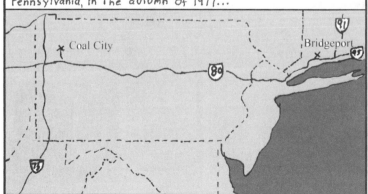

Coal City

Bridgeport

...where my mother began another criminal enterprise.

Coal City wasn't even a city but rather, according to the U.S. Census, a "populated place."

USGS
Feature Detail Report for: Coal City. Feature ID: 1172050
Name: Coal City
Class: Populated place - place or area with clustered or scattered buildings and a permanent human population: (city, settlement, town, village). A populated place is not incorporated and has no legal boundaries. See also census and civil classes.

UNITED STATES GEOLOGICAL SURVEY

The word "populated" is used here rather loosely.

Coal City was a hideaway where Mom and Carl began the process that would lead to the printing of large amounts of counterfeit money.

Camera? — Ink?
Plates? — Acid?

Check. — Check.
Check. — Check.

I was enrolled in Cranberry High School, and attended half-heartedly.

Are you going to school today?

Fine. I hope you like working for a living.

No.

Oh. You mean like you?

Their mascot was Cranberry Berry.

Both Cranberry Berry and his fellow students had very red necks. Long-haired city boys didn't go over well, although none of them ever bothered us openly.

Mark took to the woods of Pennsylvania surprisingly well, but I was plotting my return to Bridgeport.

Don't you love it here?

During the day, yes. But at night I'm climbing the fucking walls.

In the summer of 2002, I find I need distractions to keep my vow to never use heroin again, so I start hanging out in bars. Not so much to drink, but more out of sheer boredom.

You buy me a drink and later maybe I take you home.

No thanks.

The live music in these bars saves me.

From the time I was a kid, my whole family had fostered my love of music long before we learned to steal all our own records.

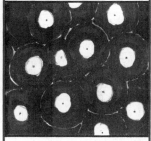

COLUMBIA House Records
Get any 12 Albums for a penny

It was John who began taking me to concerts.

Starting with Yes at the New Haven Coliseum in 1972, when I was twelve.

Followed by Traffic...

...and Jethro Tull.

The J. Geils Band

Jonny and Edgar Winter

Lynyrd Skynyrd

Aerosmith

Z.Z. Top

Black Sabbath

Neil Young

and many more

15

Including Led Zeppelin and the Rolling Stones at Madison Square Garden.

Now I turn to the usual local classic rock bar bands.

But after a few months, I discover the funk band Kneedeep.

Music kept me sane in prison.

And it's music, throughout the summer of 2002, that keeps me from returning to prison.

I work all day at my day-labor, minimum-wage job, and when I get the urge to fix, I go to a bar instead.

The difference is that I drink very little.

16

I remember once, in November of 1975, our whole family went to the New Haven Coliseum to see Bob Dylan's "Rolling Thunder Review."

Joan Baez, Joni Mitchell, Roger McGuinn, Ramblin' Jack Elliott, Kinky Friedman, Bob Neuwirth, T-Bone Burnett, Mick Ronson, David Mansfield, Steven Soles, Scarlet Rivera, Rob Stoner and Howie Wyeth, Special Guests Include Allen Ginsberg and Sam Shepard

There was me and my two brothers,

It's a family affair...

my sister and her future husband,

My family is nuts.

No shit?

and my mom with her boyfriend, Carl.

Your kids are nuts.

No shit.

We all had pretty decent seats together off the main floor.

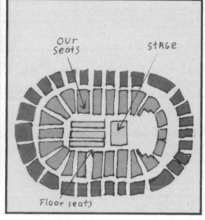

OUR SEATS

STAGE

Floor seats

I was in the habit of wandering around during the first act of concerts to see what drugs were for sale and to check out girls. The Dylan show was ideal for this.

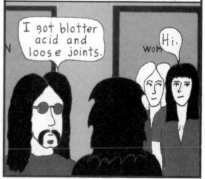

I got blotter acid and loose joints.

WOM

Hi.

When I got back to our seats at intermission, Denise told me that Carl had paid two guys $300 for their front row, center stage seats.

They got front row floor seats.

Better get up there.

I walked up there and found Carl and my mom with my brother Mark squished between them, sitting maybe ten feet from the stage.

GRATE DEAD

I bribed Mark with weed to try and get him to give up his seat.

How much pot to get your scrawny ass up?

Make me an offer.

He gave in at a quarter pound.

I'll give you an ounce?

No.

Two?

No.

Three?

No.

Four?

O.K.

I'd have easily gone up to a pound. I was that big of a Dylan fan.

You two are fucked up.

It's all right Ma...

When the musicians took the stage again, Dylan paused and eyed us.

The cloud of marijuana smoke made us easy to spot.

And we weren't your typical friend-of-the-band front-row comps.

I knew Bob when he was the unwashed phenomenon.

And I knew him when he was the original vagabond.

The only ones on that stage I'd of liked to have known better were Joni Mitchell, Joan Baez, and the exotic Scarlet Rivera.

While Mom, as might be expected, only had hormones for Dylan.

"Play 'Rolling Stone.'"

It's too hard.

We concluded that he meant it was too hard, like life, rather than too hard to play.

And he was right.

It's a hard rain...

19

Chapter 2

As a child, I was enchanted by the magic I found in books.

For a short time I sought the same magic in religion.

When that failed, it was easy to turn back to my books.

Hoffman

THE LORD OF THE RINGS
THE TWO TOWERS

STEAL THIS BOOK

Hermann Hesse
STEPPENWOLF

BRAVE NEW WORLD
ALDOUS HUXLEY

DUNE
FRANK HERBERT

THE SIRENS OF TITAN

Mika Waltar

THE EGYPTIAN

Reading books soon turned to writing.

VONNEGUT

CAT'S CRADLE

I wrote my first poem and my first short story in fifth grade and began a fantasy novel by high school, but I never took my writing too seriously.

Poems and Short story

Fantasy Novel

It just seemed like something I always did, kind of like walking.

It never occurred to me that writing could move the mind in the same way music moved the body.

Or that writing could be objectively good or bad.

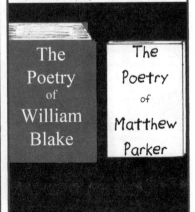

The Poetry of William Blake

The Poetry of Matthew Parker

So instead of staying in school or working hard at learning to write, I looked for shortcuts.

Are you gonna take that creative writing class?

Hell no. I already know how to write.

And found, like so many others, the illusion of magic in drugs.

LSD

I've since come to believe that Timothy Leary was wrong.

Tune in, Turn on, Drop out.

That his most famous saying was one of the stupidest things ever uttered.

I came of age in the death throes of a movement that was never my own.

R.I.P.

THE 1960s

January 1, 1960
December 31, 1969

I was born too late for the 1960s and was too radical for the peace movement.

I preferred bikers over hippies.

Fuck the Man.

Flower power.

The Velvet Underground over the Grateful Dead.

Heroin for sale.

Orange sunshine Daydream.

Let It Bleed over Let It Be.

But instead of exploding outward in relevant poetry or prose, I crawled inward, too high to write anything more than silly love poems or morbidly didactic essays.

I think that I shall never wheedle...

...a poem as lovely as a needle.

I thought that my writing was good, that I didn't need any guidance.

My teachers are Orwell and Hesse; Dylan and Jagger and Neil Young.

I may be content to listen to music without going through the difficult task of learning how to play an instrument, but I now know I can no longer do that with my writing.

THE ART OF FICTION
Henry James

For a time, the magic I found in books was enough.

As a child, it was easy enough to lose myself in fantasy books like "The Lord of the Rings" and "Dune."

Here of old was the Witch King of Angmar

MT. Gram

Harg PASS Shrine for Duke Leto II

But, like religion, magic and myth soon gave way to reality.

The New York Crimes

Nixon: "I'm not a crook"

by Gunther Gladstone

Bombings to Resume in Vietnam?

Hermann Hesse's "Steppenwolf" and "Journey to the East" taught me about spiritual outlets beyond Christianity, even though, in my early teens, I had a hard time understanding them.

Just as I did Solzhenitsyn's "The Gulag Archipelago."

Eight years hard labor for making fun of Stalin's mustache.

ZEK 71737

But this didn't stop me from reading them.

What're you reading now?

"Bury My Heart at Wounded Knee."

We had quite an array of books in our house, because, like records, we stole them.

Who'd we get this month?

Hemingway and Steinbeck.

Book clubs, like record clubs, would send out books on a "bill me later" basis.

GET ANY 6 BOOKS FOR ONLY A PENNY

Join the Bilbo Baggins Book Club Today

SEND NO MONEY NOW!

When we didn't pay, there wasn't much they could do about it, since my mom and her sisters had contracted with the book clubs using the names of us kids.

I got a threatening letter.

Me, too.

So fucking sue me.

Confiscate my big wheel.

Carlos Castaneda's "The Teachings of Don Juan" series and Aldous Huxley's "The Doors of Perception" inspired me to abuse LSD and other psychedelics.

I'm transcending Spirituality.

Ditto.

Mexican shaman high on peyote.

Famous writer high on peyote.

It took me a couple of years to figure out that these standard hippie tomes were bullshit.

HOLY COW

I burned out on LSD by the time I was 15.

Hey, little man, we're gonna take acid tonight and touch God...

...or the devil. Wanna come?

I'm done with that shit.

I then found Kurt Vonnegut on my own.

SLAUGHTERHOUSE-FIVE OR The Children's Crusade

KURT VONNEGUT, JR.

And heroin.

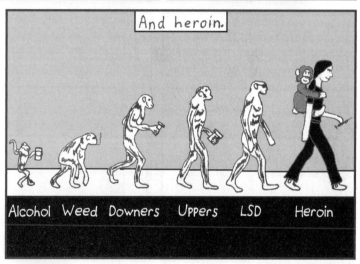

Alcohol   Weed   Downers   Uppers   LSD   Heroin

The two went well together.

Lips and lipstick

Peanut butter and jelly

Heroin and Vonnegut

Breakfast of Champions

A shot of pure nihilism to go with the senseless absurdity of living in a postmodern world.

I'm Lonely.
PERSONALS
SWM, 5'6" 150, gr br, ex con, ex junkie; I enjoy solitude, cold showers, bland food, shiny objects, sharp objects, waiting in lines, cafeterias, and I will do just about anything for a pack of non-filter Camels.
Further background info can be had at:
http://www.bop.gov/
http://www.adc.State.az

Women ain't exactly beating a path to my door.

"I saw him first."

"No! He's my excon."

"I want to lick his tattoos."

All that shtick about women loving outlaws is utter bullshit. This is especially true for a guy who has little to offer beyond a colorful and lengthy criminal past.

"I love bad boys."

"Good. Here's a copy of my criminal record."

"Oh my. That's too long. Sorry, but I don't date beyond misdemeanants."

I have a terrible job, no car, no bank account, no credit card, and, at age 42, I still live at home with my mom.

"Hello, ladies."

Who is herself miserable, waiting for heroin to pull me back in, for that collect call from the county jail. Again.

"Can I borrow twenty bucks?"

"He's using again."

"You have a collect call from the Madison Street Jail. If you accept the charges, please press one."

But I try to improve my situation: When school starts in August, I work hard, and after a month of classes, I get my financial aid money, which I use to pay off the roughly $3,000 in traffic fines I had when I got out of prison last March.

"Nice work, Mr. Parker."

A+

New bank account

BANK

FAFSA cash

COURT

Massive fines

It takes me a week to visit all the different courts and pay off all my different fines to get my license reinstated.

	courts to visit
✓	Scottsdale City Court
✓	Phoenix Municipal Court
✓	Mesa City Court
✓	Central Phoenix Justice Court
✓	Northwest Phoenix Justice Court
✓	East Phoenix Justice Court No. 1

Meanwhile, I do remarkably well in my first semester at Scottsdale Community College and am made an honor student the following semester.

Mr. Parker, we are honored to honor your newfound honesty.

It's an honor to be honored thus. I feel just like a trustee.

ΦBK
PHI BETA KAPPA

I can't help wondering if they'd have done this if they knew about my secret thoughts concerning Rush.

Also in my second semester I get a job at the college TV station...

MCTV
MARICOPA COMMUNITY COLLEGES TELEVISION

You're a carpenter?

More or less.

You're hired.

...and switch majors from journalism to English Lit.

Write me some obituaries.

Write me a paper on Shakespeare's "Hamlet."

It's been a year since my release, and I celebrate alone.

MARCH 19, 2003

I just did two years on a two-and-a-half-year sentence for felony shoplifting.

March 2000
Su M Tu W Th Fr Sa
1 2 3 4
5 6 7 8 9 10 11
12 13 14 15 16 17 18
19 20 21 22 23 24 25
26 27 28 29 30 31

March 2001
Su M Tu W Th F Sa
1 2 3
4 5 6 7 8 9 10
11 12 13 14 15 16 17
18 19 20 21 22 23 24
25 26 27 28 29 30 31

March 2002
Su M Tu W Th F Sa
1 2
3 4 5 6 7 8 9
10 11 12 13 14 15 16
17 18 19 20 21 22 23
24 25 26 27 28 29 30
31

I'd been stealing cigarettes from convenience stores...

How much for those aspirin?

Which ones?

...and selling them to support my heroin habit.

I've got 25 packs at a buck a pack.

I'll take them all.

I only used twice in the last two years I was locked up.

You fixing this weekend?

No. I'm almost done with that shit.

ADOC *ADOC*

Once on Christmas of 2000...

Deck the walls with shanks and needles, fa la la la la la la la la,

---

...and my birthday of 2001.

Happy birthday to you, You live in a Zoo, You look like a junkie...

Twice in two years. And this from a guy who used to fix every day, twice before breakfast.

Are we gonna eat, or what?

Soon as I'm done here.

The effort I used to put into getting and staying high combined with the natural buzz that engulfs me when released from Prison leaves me with a lot of excess energy...

Excuse me, sir, but you seem to be humming.

SCOTTSDALE COMMUNITY COLLEGE Financial Aid Dept.

... Which I simply channel into my studies.

It works remarkably well.

Extra reading

Extra writing

Extra rereading and rewriting

Extra credit

A+

In my second year at SCC I decide to try to fulfill my childhood dream by applying to Columbia University. My writing is improving, and I feel that at Columbia it will improve even more.

Columbia / GS
Ideal for adults who wish to pursue an Ivy League education.

♛ application for admissions I

Mail completed form and $50 applicatio
Office of Admissions and Financial Aid
School of General Studies, Columbia U
408 Lewisohn Hall, Mail Code 4101
2970 Broadway
New York, NY 10027

program information
Fall (September) Year _2005_ Early Acti
_____ Early Action Summer (May) Yea
International Student International Stude
Regular Decision Regular Decision
Deadlines

But when the administrators of those hallowed ivy halls inform me that they need my latest SAT scores, I march into the office of Sandy, my creative writing professor, and throw myself into a chair.

What in the fuck is an SAT?

She's amused.

It's a college admissions exam taken by high school students.

I'm confused.

You did go to high school, didn't you?

No.

I explain to her how I got my GED in federal prison in 1988...

High School Equivalency Diploma
Awarded to

Matthew Parker
Number 19972-008

By the United States Bureau of Prisons and the State of California

Federal Prison Camp, Boron, CA

...but had never taken an SAT.

Well, you're going to have to take one now.

I tell her I'll look into it.

I'll be back.

But in looking into it I find that I can't take the SAT before the application deadline.

Columbia University/GS

All applications due by: 12/10/2003

Scholastic Aptitude Test (SAT)

Next testing date: 12/15/2003

I'm furious, and spend an afternoon cursing what I see as an alliance between academia and bureaucracy.

Mother-fuckin' cock-suckin' son of a mother-fuckin' whore god-damned pieces of bureaucratic shit.

The following day I march back into Sandy's office and throw myself into the same chair, still cussing.

Son of a fucking SAT sucking...

In response, she makes a phone call and finds that Columbia offers its own entry exam that I can take, in lieu of the SAT.

Hello? Admissions office? My name is Sandy and I'm an alumnus...

She then calls her travel agent...

Hello? Yes? This is Sandy. Good. How are you? Wonderful...

...and books me a flight to New York City...

... yes. Roundtrip, Phoenix to JFK. No, nonstop. Umm, not sure. Hold on.

Will Thursday do?

... slicing through the red tape with the expediency of cash.

Wonderful. Thank you. Please mail me the bill.

My propensity for four-letter words melts away into a soft patter of gibbering humility.

There now. Wasn't that simple?

I like flowers and puppies.

A couple of days later I'm back in her office. Sandy tells me stories about her time at Columbia, and, as we talk, she hands me 300 dollars.

Spending money.

Panel 1:

I'm stunned into a very rare silence.

Panel 2:

My vocal cords, puzzled by the lack of direction from my brain, look to my balls.

Help us out up here, you two nuts.

FUCK CENSORSHIP

Panel 3:

This is a common maneuver, designed to override speechlessness with oozing machismo...

Hold on. We're sending up some choice four-letter words.

Panel 4:

...but with an effort of will I manage to deflect the testosterone-laced words rising from my nether regions...

How about "mother fucking"?

Why do you always have to pick "cock sucking"?

We do all the work.

Yeah. I'd like to see him cum without us...

And "cock sucking"?

Because he's a lazy fuck.

While he gets all the credit.

...or swear.

Panel 5:

...and blurt out:

I can't take this. You've already done too much.

Yes you can.

No, I can't.

Panel 6:

We argue back and forth for a while, until she says:

Matthew, take it. Don't you think you deserve it? You work harder than anyone else.

FUCK

Panel 7:

I took her point, along with the money.

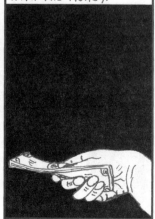

Panel 8:

But a plan to even the score had already formed in my head.

All right. But I have ways of paying you back.

FUCK

29

I know that the best way to pay Sandy back is to become a successful writer.

#1 Best Seller

Matthew Parker

PINK FLOYD

Since that seems unlikely, I begin a portrait of Jim Morrison for her.

But despite my artistic talents, my real love lies in writing, mostly poetry.

It's open-mike night at Rula Bulas, Walt Richardson's ballad pierces my eyes like the forgotten Morning Stars setting over the desert.

The obligatory Budweiser sits like a sentinel over the leafy Camels; barbs growing smartly from the rose-tinted table to settle smartly in calloused skin.

The waitress smiles sweetly, but sees only a worn-out tip. She delivers the apple pie sitting like a brown-sugar island in a white boy sea, so distinct from the bitter taste of heroin knocking at my twice-baked door.

I wrote hundreds of poems while in jail or prison.

But Sandy's class incorporates fiction as well, and she encourages me to move beyond the limits of poetry.

Fiction Nonfiction

POETRY PRISON

Break out.

Nor is she the first.

Don't you ever write anything else?

On my last prison sentence I worked with Writer Richard Shelton at a prison in Tucson in September of 2001.

Arizona State Prison Complex Tucson
Manzanita Unit
Is Offering Creative Writing Classes
with Author Richard Shelton
No Regis[...] required
Every Sa[...] :00 a.m.
Concentrat[...] nd Poetry

Richard was director of the Creative Writing Program and the University of Arizona Poetry Center, as well as the author of a number of books of poetry and nonfiction, including the award-winning "Going Back to Bisbee."

A

Going Back to Bisbee

Richard Shelton

Knowing the healing power inherent in writing, he's been running the prison writing workshop as a volunteer for 20 years.

My own writing has helped me to heal over the years.

Poetry
essays
fiction
nonfiction
art exercise

Richard also publishes an annual literary journal written exclusively by Arizona state prison inmates or former inmates.

And not only can your writing help you, but others, as well, if and when it's published.

Poetry
essays
fiction
nonfiction
art exercise

It's called the "Walking Rain Review."

Walking Rain
Review IX

He and Sandy have worked together.

You know Richard Shelton?

Small world.

I sure do.

It is. Kind of like a prison, ain't it?

Richard also pushed me away from poetry toward essays.

Your poetry is pretty dismal. How 'bout writing me an expository essay?

A what essay?

Didactic
istent
ihilist

Thanks to folks like Richard and Sandy, I now know my writing needs lots of work.

Revision, revision, fucking revision.

My poetry and essays have thus far been rejected by "Walking Rain."

Dear Matthew,
We regret to inform you that we have determined that your writing is not suitable for WRR at this time.
Sincerely,
The Editors

P.S. This standard rejection letter, in combo with other rejection letters and/or traffic tickets, makes for some great wallpaper.

So now I'm more eager than ever to get to Columbia and study under the best teachers possible.

COLUMBIA/GS
School of General Studies
Faculty

Featuring

Some famous writers and even more famous professors

Contact your admissions office today.

I also know that living in New York City itself will provide me with oodles of inspiration.

...and this is where Dylan and Ginsberg met.

On the flight to New York, it occurs to me that this is my first vacation in 15 years.

My last was when I went back to Connecticut from Arizona in 1987...

...but since I was on the run from the United States Marshals, I don't count that one.

U.S. District Court for the District of Arizona.
Fugitive of Justice
Bench Warrant
Issued for: Matthew Parker
CR-86-00210-02
FBI No: 548 904 CA5
DOB: 04/05/1960
POB: Bridgeport, CT
Issued by: The Honorable Charles L. Hardy

Having been born and raised in Bridgeport, Connecticut, I thought it would be the perfect place to hide.

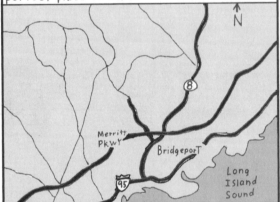

Heroin was the dictator of my higher brain functions at the time.

On this more recent trip, my higher brain functions are dominated by sex.

Should I spend some of Sandy's $300 on a hooker?

I still haven't found a woman who loves outlaws.

In the past, I didn't even have luck with hookers.

Most of the girlfriends I had while a junkie were prostitutes.

And not one of them had, like Julia Roberts, a heart of gold

...and they were all, to a woman, only slightly less scandalous than titty dancers.

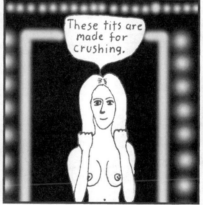

But in truth it's intimacy, rather than sex, that I crave most.

I'm suffering from touch deprivation...

ARIZONA DEPARTMENT OF CORRECTIONS
Rules for Visitation

NO HUGS ALLOWED

Except for quickies at both the commencement and termination of each respective visit

Violaters subject to disciplinary action

...a very common malady amongst convicts or, in my case, an ex con-vict who would be very happy with just one of these mythical women who supposedly love outlaws.

Or women who love real outlaws, anyway, which, by my last count, happens to be none of them.

WORLD PERSONALS
1.5 BILLION SINGLE WOMEN LOOKING FOR LOVE AND INTIMACY*

*No one with felony convictions need apply. DUIs and other misdemeanors are OK.

I could buy sex, but I couldn't buy intimacy...

...at least not for $300.

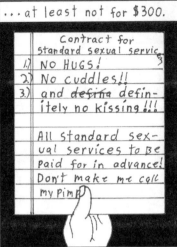

It gives a whole new meaning to the saying "Hugs, not drugs," don't it?

Instead, once I get to New York City, I go to Dock's Oyster Bar on 89th and Broadway and have a lobster dinner and a glass of expensive red wine.

It feels good to touch lips and tongue to something soft and yielding.

I then go back to my tiny room and jerk off.

Some things never change.

34

On my way up to Columbia the following day I stop at Strawberry Fields.

CENTRAL PARK W.

W 72 st.

I haven't been to Central Park since John Lennon was killed back in 1980.

≣ The New York Crimes ≣

December 9, 1980

John Lennon shot and killed in front of Dakota

Ucillore rantest, qui derendit, volum velesequetem ererovit et inalles et quo volorpo ratur, que doluptaquat moloribus at accus suntem fugauit, consequid que veniuquo tecum et aut utenimi ncuuto consenis

est molupit laes, jum vitia debis aut inctatur, sandi dolut aceperibuuci berum delit ea et omnimus tissita tinsdam sunsquam aceserit aut et hilinsectitore sus aut voluptatemis exorem quuntis um fagitam

fagiat maxim ut quam qis ut dolesitem. Nihicia temporum nisuit facit porro ina doluption esti is aut estiurem. Equuam quas cicidus anducia oceprehonis num quis oatibus undaut. Ferat qui ad ut quis dolorant

Lone gunman apprehended

Nobistenp eliquatese volaptat ma das, omnihil laborporepe eccatus, tenulpuam ut et ex eosi officia nam landiisncia consequiam qui arcilignatis conos expedit oram commimp eribuss cum quibus dolorem

porastum quos nis dolo qui tentar? Quiatur? Icim qui blatia vellend aectem volaptu capta velestibus et asperuptur rescitinis aut et harcit laturiam, consectar ati ist, sequam eac necea apelgus imimut runqui delia

Vigil for Lennon to be held Sunday in Central Park

Alitae. Nam quam ut eostis estorectem rom vent, offic tet atum ipilse consequamus estor autenis idempos dolut accus aut fugias re, astemporro elenem

quis santredus aliquaestium et a volam volorro blah incidus ciusup tationis cruptat espla doleruis, volligus ipsapid modici dolo peribea

Then I was with two hippie girls...

...and was broke, freezing, and feeling the first pangs of heroin withdrawal.

You OK, baby?

No. I'm sick.

How much farther?

As we attended Lennon's vigil, I cursed the fates, knowing that some of the best China White in the country was just a few blocks away.

This is so moving.

I wish I was in Harlem.

Fuck it's cold.

Now I squat there, on my heels and away from the tourists.

I spot a squirrel...

...and it strikes me that this is the first squirrel I've seen in 15 years.

Welcome to Arizona

No Squirrels, lots of Lizards

He's being industrious and wants no truck with memorials.

I squat there, listening to the traffic and sirens and blaring horns drifting in from Central Park West...

... an auditory memoriam of a world I've wandered into the park to escape.

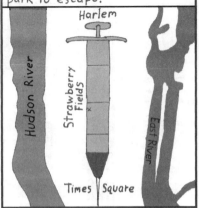

I smoke a cigarette, then head up to Columbia.

The test is all English. Just reading and writing and a short essay.

Columbia/GS School of General Studies
Entry Exam for Dummies*

*If you can read, please proceed to page 2.

1

It's ridiculously easy.

Read question completely before answering

1.) Spell "spelling."

2.) Read "reading."

3.) Write "writing."

(25-point bonus question) Write an essay about "essaying."

Just like that silly GED test I took in federal prison back in 1988.

1.) What does "GED" stand for?

2.) What does "equivalency" mean?

3.) Please finish the following sentence: "All men are created_____."

On the subway ride back to my hotel, I'm thinking about hookers again.

I only actually paid for sex one time.

I mean, we're paying for it one way or another.

I was on parole in Scottsdale in 1993, and had a tracking bracelet on my ankle.

Real. Comfortable. Ankle bracelet.

If I wasn't home from work by 7:00pm the bracelet would alert the authorities to my truancy.

PAROLE TRACKING CENTER

I'd be tracked down, arrested, and dragged back to prison.

Bet you'll never be late from work again, you worthless criminal.

It was a way to get the damn thing off my ankle...

Well, at least you're off home arrest.

...but not the preferred way.

Congratulations! You're off home arrest. You may now frolic freely with whomever you fancy.

In an effort to avoid this and satisfy my lust, I left work early...

Gotta split at two o'clock today, boss. Personal issues.

No problem.

...and picked up a hooker.

Ooo. I love men on home arrest.

She was tall and blonde with big tits, the exact opposite of the type of women I was attracted to.

Blonde
light eyes — Thin lips
Pale skin — Big tits
Big hands
Long, supermodel feet

Brunette
Dark eyes — Thick lips
Dark skin — Little tits
Tiny hands
Small, cute feet

I hate big tits...

The perfect breast fits in a champagne glass, oui?

FRANCE

...but she only charged me 40 bucks to touch them and any other part of her body.

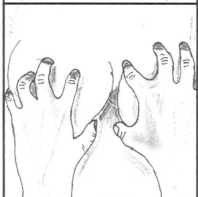

I'd just been in prison for three calendar years.

Once in the hotel I was completely naked in a matter of seconds...

Wow. That was quick.

I'll likely cum even quicker.

...except for the ankle bracelet and a condom.

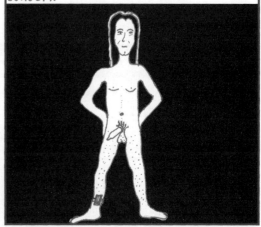

I climbed on top of her and started pumping while sucking on those huge melons.

I gave myself three minutes. Tops.

She immediately began moaning in feigned rapture.

Oh you're so big. Oooo you feel so good.

This had the opposite effect of the one intended...

Oh yeah oooo harder baby, fuck me, fuck me harder.

...in that my dick immediately shrunk to the size of a shotgun shell.

I pushed myself up with my arms and looked down at her.

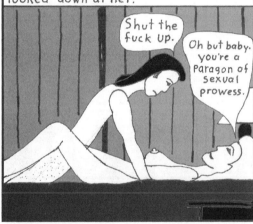

Shut the fuck up.

Oh but baby. You're a paragon of sexual prowess.

She pretended to be hurt.

Look. All you have to do is lie there. You don't gotta pretend you're enjoying this. Just be quiet and let me get my nut.

Sure, baby.

But when I started up again she did the same thing.

Ohhh baby. Oooooooooo gigantor.

I stopped, pulled on my pants...

I'll be right back.

Ok, baby.

...and went out to my truck and shot a speedball that I had stashed under the dashboard, then went back into the room.

Oooooo baby.

The good thing about heroin was that it made my dick harder than Chinese arithmetic.

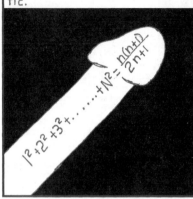

$$1^2 + 2^2 + 3^2 + \cdots + N^2 = \frac{n(n+1)}{2n+1}$$

The bad thing was that while on it I couldn't possibly get a nut.

This was not a good scenario for a prostitute.

Are you cumming?

Oh yeah.

After 15 odd minutes of my going at her, manic as a pile driver, she figured out I was lying and pushed me off.

Get off.

She was pissed off, and showed it, but I was enjoying myself.

Jesus, I'm fucking raw. I won't be able to work for the rest of the night.

High as a kite, I no longer cared that my semen was still imprisoned.

She dressed quickly and asked me for a ride, I obliged, lecturing her the whole way.

It's your own fault. All you had to do was keep your mouth shut...

...and let me get my nut. But no. You had to pretend you were enjoying it.

Panel 1: Ten years later I get off the subway, thinking about this...

Panel 2: ...and go up to my room and jerk off. Again.

Panel 3: A few days later I return to Arizona and, a month after that, I get the rejection letter.

Columbia University School of General Studies
408 Lewisohn Hall, MC4101
2970 Broadway
New York, NY 10027

...tthew Parker
74th St.
...tsdale, AZ 85257

Panel 4: They want me to reapply next fall.

COLUMBIA G/S
School of General Studies

Standard Rejection Letter

Dear Matthew Parker,
We do not believe that you are a good candidate for Columbia's School of General Studies at this time. However, we would like you to apply again for the fall 2004 semester.
Sincerely,

Panel 5: Columbia is concerned about my math scores.

Grade Transcripts for Matthew Parker

Algebra 092   D

Algebra 092 (Redux)   C

Chinese Arithmetic   A+

Panel 6: They tell me to take another algebra class, get at least a B, and reapply.

Future Grade Transcript for Matthew Parker.*

Algebra 120   B+

Chinese Arithmetic   A+

*This grade transcript is non-corporeal and can therefore only exist in an Einstein-Rosen Bridge.

$$r_s = \frac{2GM}{c^2}$$

Panel 7: I register for one at SCC for the first summer session of 2004.

ALGEBRA 120

Please note: The determination of your grade will be governed by Heisenberg's Uncertainty Principle. To wit:

$$\Delta x \, \Delta p \geq \frac{\hbar}{2}$$

Panel 8: Algebra doesn't compute. To me it isn't practical simply because I don't understand it.

$$\left[\frac{1}{2m}\left(\vec{\sigma}\cdot(\vec{p}-q\vec{A})\right)^2+q\phi\right]|\psi\rangle = i\hbar\frac{\partial}{\partial t}|\psi\rangle$$

$$i\hbar\partial_t\psi_\pm = \left(\frac{(\vec{p}-q\vec{A})^2}{2\,2m}+q\phi\right)\hat{l}\psi_\pm - \frac{qh}{2m}\vec{\sigma}\cdot\vec{B}\psi_\pm$$

$$E\Psi = H\Psi$$

Note: For a more applicable interpretation of the above formulas, please see "Schrödinger's cat."

Panel 9: Except for pitch. I used pitch as a carpenter to cut rafters for roofs.

And stringers for stairways. How much does the Slope of a stairway or roof rise per foot? That's pitch.

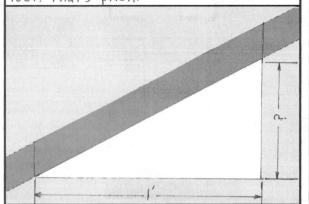

But I see no practical use for, say, quadratic equations. I'm certain there is one, but I can't seem to do equations beyond the simple formula for pitch.

This is the formula for a quadratic equation:

$$\frac{-b \pm \sqrt{b^2 - 4ac}}{2a} = X$$

Seems simple enough, don't it?

And this is the formula for rise per foot, or pitch.

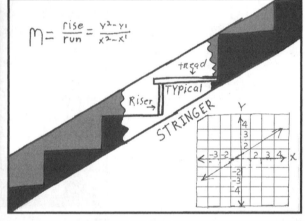

$$m = \frac{rise}{run} = \frac{y^2 - y_1}{x^2 - x^1}$$

tread

Typical

riser

STRINGER

And this is the formula I use for staying clean in my first year out of prison.

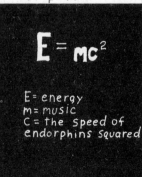

$$E = mc^2$$

E = energy
m = music
C = the speed of endorphins squared

Where my own energy is equal to music times the speed of endorphins squared.

Admittedly not as quick as heroin, but in the long haul just as effective.

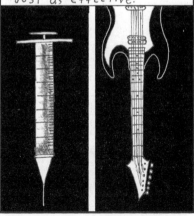

Three months after my mom moved us to the wilds of Pennsylvania, I hitched a ride with a family friend back to Connecticut.

I wish you'd change your mind and stay, and especially stay the fuck in school.

I know, Mom. But I can't take it here anymore.

Bridgeport was a sleazy town, but at least it had paved roads, convenience stores, and a modicum of tolerance.

EAST Side PACKAGE STORE

We'll sell liquor to ANYONE

OPEN

DELI
sandwiches   mea

SE HABLA ESPANOL

Jeremiah Johnson I wasn't, nor wanted to be.

Has anyone seen my goddamned Grizz?

Once I was back in Connecticut, I got a job as an apprentice machinist.

Mohawk Tool & Die

A few months later, in April of 1978, I turned 18. To celebrate, a girl named Diane picked me up.

You're too easy.

And, uninvited, moved into my little closet with me the next day.

Since your clothes are here I'm assuming you're also here? For good?

Yes. My brothers threw me out of the house.

She then entreated me to get her pregnant.

Knock me up, baby.

Are you crazy?

43

Every night she'd plead.

Oh please. I just want a baby. No strings. No bullshit. I'll move out if you want me to and never chase you for support...

After two weeks I finally said yes.

...I'll take total responsibility for the child. No one will ever even know your name...

Ok. Ok. O-fucking-k...

Just to shut her up.

...but only if you have a boy.

Ok.

And, of course, she did.

It's a boy!

My son was born in December of 1978, and I gave Diane a crash course in welfare fraud.

You have to tell them you don't know where or even who the father is.

STATE of CONNECTICUT DEPARTMENT SOCIAL ... ICES

Welfare and Food Stamp ...

We also got married so we could file taxes jointly. Anything for a few extra bucks.

I now pronounce you...

In the interim, my sister, Denise, had graduated from college, got married, and moved to Arizona.

Congratulations.

Thank you and goodbye.

My mother, her boyfriend, Carl, and my brother Mark soon followed.

Printing Press?

Ink?

Weed?

Check.

Check.

Check.

44

My brother John was sent upstate a few months after I had met Diane.

Somers State Prison
Connecticut
Department of
Corrections

Keep off the Grass

I'd often visit him in the county jail, before he was sent to Prison.

North Avenue Jail
Fairfield County
Bridgeport, Connecticut

I hated going into that fucking place and was always relieved to get out.

Soooo? What's new?

?

Nowhere did I get a greater sense of his utter homelessness than in that county jail.

How is it in there?

I'd rather be living on the streets in winter.

As well as, in an odd way, my own.

I can't find my way home...

That cruddy jail was his home, and if released he had nowhere to go.

So what will you do when you get out?

Beats me.

Nor did I.

IRFIELD COUNTY

Home is overrated.

uses

Homer's

ents

Real

ces

Estate

Our home, such as it was, had been uprooted and moved to a desert 2,500 miles away.

AINS

Welcome to
OLD TOWN
SCOTTSDALE

A place neither of us had ever been to for more than a few days.

Well, when you get out, you can stay with Diane and me.

Cool. Just for a week or two.

45

When we were kids, John had always been there for me.

That kid fucking with you?

A little.

You want me to fuck him up?

Naw. I can handle it.

All right. But I'm here if you need me.

I know.

He showed me how to control a boat at sea.

No. Turn into the wave.

And how to ride a motorcycle.

He taught me how to take things apart, figure out what's wrong with them, and put them back together.

See how the rings are torn up on this piston?

Yes.

It's losing too much compresion in the cylinder. Slows the bike.

John had an innate engineering sense...

You're going to need a crossbeam under the left side for support. Otherwise it might collapse.

...and was a natural thief.

You run a hotwire from the battery to the coil, then jump the solenoid with a screwdriver, and...

"VRAVROOM"

I once helped him steal a Porsche engine and wheel it home in a shopping cart.

It was because of John that we never paid a gas bill. On the rare occasions when the utilities man got into our house and locked our gas off, John would simply break the lock and turn it back on.

He also taught me how to ice skate and play hockey...

...and saved my dog, Jake, from drowning when Jake fell through thin ice near where the stream ran into the pond.

He's drowning!

Stay back. I'll get him.

John lay down, spread-eagle, and broke the ice with a hockey stick until he could reach him.

We'd also sneak into Remington Woods, the ammunition dump disguised as a nature preserve.

DANGER
No Trespassing
Violators Will Be
Prosecuted

Remington Woods was 420 acres of wilderness fenced off with barbed wire and protected by roving security guards in station wagons.

The fence line ran right through our backyard.

Trespassing in Remington Woods was our first venture into crime and was one of the few crimes I was ever comfortable committing.

47

Around 1972 John and some friends started a street gang and used the two-car garage in our backyard as a clubhouse.

"We need to organize..."

"...and protect..."

"...our criminal activity."

They flew their colors on sleeveless denim jackets...

"We..."

"...have become..."

"...territorial."

...and had forged ties with the Savage Skulls out of the Bronx.

They protected their territory by not doing crimes in our neighborhood.

"Why don't we do some burglaries around here?"

"Because you don't shit where you sleep."

It was about this time, when I was 13, that I started selling pot.

"20 bucks an ounce, four for 70."

"I'll take a dime bag."

John kept me at a distance from the gang's burglary, car stealing, and occasional armed robbery.

"Let's do some houses up around White Plains Road today. No need to bring Matthew."

This was fine with me. I wasn't at ease with most crimes, except selling pot, which was different. I saw it as natural.

"If it grows on the earth, it was meant to be sold, right?"

Like wandering around Remington Woods.

48

Initially, it was John who was chosen to sell small amounts of pot.

Here's a pound. You pay the house $150 for it. Got it?

No problem.

The business began when my mom's new boyfriend, Carl, moved into our house.

Hey, kid. Where can I get some THC?

Beats me.

He had the connections in Arizona.

The Mexican "Mean Green" Connection

TO JFK

Phoenix — SCOTTSDALE

SKY HArbor AIRPORT

TUCSON

MEXICO

NOGALES

But John was a poor salesman. He was always too high or drunk, to where he actually lost money.

Let's see. That's five nickels and two dimes, no...

So the business was handed over to me.

John, you're out. Matthew, you're in.

I took to it in the same way John took to stealing cars.

20 bucks. Next.

But John was jealous of my success. He became belligerent, even violent, when drunk or high on barbiturates.

I'm the one who should be selling weed. I'm the oldest.

You have your car theft and burglaries.

So, fueled by drugs and alcohol, we started getting into horrendous fights.

These fights not only brought disruption to our already active household, but sometimes the cops, as well.

BPT POLICE

49

From 1973 on, John started getting arrested regularly— everything from auto theft to disturbing the peace.

As if my mom didn't already have enough on her plate.

I need 50 pounds for Jose, 25 for Seaman...

Not only was she smuggling 150 pounds of weed across the country every couple weeks...

Two checked bags, please.

...but she was stealing pot from Carl when she cut the kilos into pounds...

Ten pounds for Carl, one for Matthew. Ten...

...and skimming money from the take.

Four of these $10,000 stacks are short.

Huh. Must've miscounted.

All of which kept me awake nights.

Oh, God, please don't let my mom get busted at the airport, or robbing Carl, or...

On top of all this, she had to deal with extorting bikers...

We want 10 percent of your take.

Go fuck yourselves. How's that for a percent?

...a continuation of welfare fraud...

Why collect welfare still? Don't we have enough money?

Matthew. We can never have enough money.

...and her boyfriend, Carl, who wasn't too stable.

What the hell IS wrong with him?

Bad acid trip.

So John being uncontrollable and bringing cops to the house was more than she could handle.

"I'm fed up. You have to move out."

"Fine. I don't need you."

BAD CO

He was the first of us out on the streets, ending up there by the end of 1975.

EAST PACKAGE DEL BEER WINE FINE SPIRITS
Patent Medici

It was sad to see him out there, wandering from high to high...

"Got an extra beer, guys?"

"Can I get a hit off that joint?"

"Any bootleg ludes for sale?"

...and I know that it broke my mother's heart...

...but he had little trouble surviving.

"Hey. I haven't seen you for a while. Do you need anything?"

"Naw. I'm getting by."

Most of my mother's life was a struggle to keep us off the streets while, at the same time, preparing us for that eventuality.

For most of my childhood, at least up until the time we started selling pot, she was just a step or two ahead of the bill collectors and terrified that they'd catch her.

Phone
GAS

So she prepared us for if and when it might happen.

"And never steal bologna when roast beef is available. The crime and punishment is the same for both."

So when John was released from prison in the autumn of 1979, I made sure he didn't have to live on the streets.

He lived with me and my new family for a time before deciding to move out to Arizona.

I hate this fucking town. I'm thinking of moving west.

?

?

?

I thought it was a bad idea and told him so.

What the fuck are you gonna do out there?

Yes!

Don't know. But can it be any worse than here?

John hadn't changed much. In his mind it was easier to move across the country than to just get a job in Bridgeport.

You can find work here, you know. It makes no sense to go to Arizona.

I know. But I'm sick of the cold, sick of this whole town.

He left in late November.

LOS ANGELES

WOLF

By the first of February, he was dead.

Matthew, does John have any tattoos?

No.

Are you sure?

Yes. Why?

They found a body. They think it's your brother John.

Well, is it?

I don't know. This body has no tattoos. Are you sure John has no tattoos?

I'm sure.

All right. But I'm going to find out for sure. I'll call you back.

OK.

52

Chapter 3

In jail or prison, you have to adapt to survive. I learned this on my first prison sentence, served from 1987 to 1989, for dealing in counterfeit bills. I did my time in the county jail as well as various prisons in both Arizona and California.

| Maricopa County Jail |
| Federal Correctional Institution, Terminal Island |
| Federal Prison Camp, Boron |
| Federal Correctional Institution, Phoenix |

This was reinforced on my second and third prison terms, mostly served in the Arizona State Prison, Perryville. It was there where I learned that you have to play dumb on a grand scale in order to blend in.

What's the capital of Africa?

Beats me.

If, like me, you're a white male, you have to pretend you're a racist to avoid violent repercussions.

You have to hate Jews first, then niggers, and spics, and ragheads, and Chinks...

Oh I do, I do.

Don't ever suggest that natural selection is a viable theory, or that DNA has proven that we are all, as a species, very closely related.

You do realize that all human DNA is 99 percent identical?

Niggers, too?

Try not to appear overly literate or intellectually eloquent.

And I hate to point out the obvious, but you're all in fact moribund sycophants of an antiquated philosophy.

Facism = Hitler Mussolini the Klan

Marxism an the Spanish Civil War

Make believe that Hitler was a swell guy who was only doing what comes natural or you'll be cut out of the herd and devoured.

Hitler, man? It was just survival of the fittest, you know?

You bet.

WHITE PRIDE

What's most disturbing is that the herd mentality that rules the language of the incarcerated is merely a microcosm of our own society, our own disparate factions and dearth of eloquence.

Anyone engaging in illegal financial transactions will be caught and persecuted.

And childrens do learn.

In this sense, we are all doing life without parole.

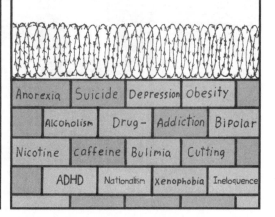

Anorexia	Suicide	Depression	Obesity
Alcoholism	Drug-	Addiction	Bipolar
Nicotine	Caffeine	Bulimia	Cutting
ADHD	Nationalism	Xenophobia	Ineloquence

In prison, I was called a baby lifer; the guy with a little bit of time to do, always serving a sentence under five years (also called wino time).

How much time you'd get?

I got more time in sitting on the toilet.

Two years.

Then there's the bitch, or punk. These are derogatory terms denoting femininity or homosexuality. If another prisoner calls you a bitch, you have to fight him, or else you're admitting you're a bitch.

Have you ever cried during a movie?

Good man.

No. And I slap my girlfriend when she cries.

A Bullet is a nickname applied to a young prisoner sent out on missions to assault anyone his superiors aim him at. A bullet's motive is to work his way up the gang hierarchy.

Pay your dope debt.

Caucasians are white men who are not overtly racist. It's considered an insult to be called a Caucasian by a white boy/Peckerwood.

Can't we all just get along?

A Chican is a derogatory term for a Mexican American.

Hola. I mean Hello.

Chief means a Native American.

How? In the fuck?

Child molesters are cho mos or baby rapers.

Sugar and spice and...

The correct term for a prison guard is corrections officer, or CO for short, because prisons are theoretically geared toward correcting criminal behavior in prisoners before they're released.

Is your behavior being corrected, Parker?

My bad.

Not in the slightest.

Slang terms for CO's include bull, COP, hack, PO-PO, PO-lease, screw, turd (so-called because of their brown uniforms), and turnkey.

Technically, we are not COPS.

I stand corrected.

ALL INMATES MUST BE CUFFED

Most prisoners apply the word convict to themselves. "Convict" has a certain honor and code; i.e, macho, non-snitching, and most often racist. Calling a convict an inmate is considered an insult, since inmate implies that that prisoner has no honor or code and so is, therefore, weak.

I'm a convict.

I'm a convict.

I'm a convict.

I'm a vegan.

I'm a convict.

When taking a shit in jail or PRISON, you must Perform a courtesy flush. This is the Practice of flushing the toilet as soon as your shit hits the water in an effort to reduce the shitty odor.

KERWHOOSH!

KERWHOOSH!

A new and inexperienced inmate is called a fish.

Hi. I've just arrived. Can you tell me where the golf course is, please?

?

The slang term for disciplinary segregation is the hole.

30 days in the hole.

A hustle is a way to make money in prison. Doing legal work for other prisoners is a hustle; so is selling artwork or drugs.

Legal work here.

Art for Sale.

Loose joints. Heroin.

I was considered an independent because I wouldn't clique up with a gang. Independents are respected as long as they don't snitch and/or cross preset racial barriers.

Using drugs intravenously is often referred to as "In the Spoon." When being released, there's a cliché that states, "Out the gate at eight, in the spoon by noon."

Your jacket is your past criminal history, or record.

Keester is slang for hiding drugs and other contraband in the anal cavity, aka the safe.

Lifers are serving a life sentence with or without the possibility of parole.

Off brand is a derogatory term used by white boys to describe anyone who is nonwhite.

Being charged with a new crime while already locked up in jail or prison is called a page two.

Paper is a slang term for probation or parole. Being on paper means that, after your release, you're still under the jurisdiction (and therefore the rules) of the jail or prison you were released from and can be sent back for violating any of them.

PC is short for protective custody, aka punk city.

Peckerwood is a derogatory term for a poor white Southerner and was adopted by white boys with pride as a mark of racial distinction.

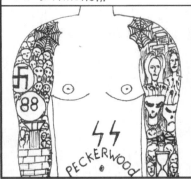

Paisa is a derogatory term for a Mexican national, akin to wetback.

Sancho is the universal name for the guy who is fucking your wife or girlfriend while you're doing your time.

I can't get a hold of my ol' lady.

Of course not. She's with Sancho.

You'll be called a rabbit if you have escapes and/or attempted escapes in your criminal history, or rabbit in your jacket.

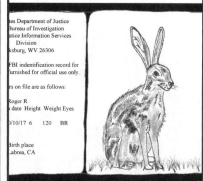

A street-to-street is a system of paying for drugs whereby you send a letter to your family/friends on the street and instruct them to mail a money order for the amount you owe for the drugs to the dealer's family/friends.

Matthew Parker 87078
Arizona State Prison
Complex - Yuma
Cocopah Unit

Kim Courier
75 Circle St.
Phoenix, AZ
85001

An elevation of rank, or stripe, often appears in the form of a tattoo (Nazi insignia for white boys), given to a bullet or other convict who has completed a mission successfully.

Congrats on your first stripe.

Thanks. Hold fucking still.

Swasi is a tattoo of a swastika. Swasis must be earned - you can't just ask for one.

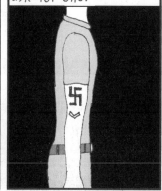

Turtle is a slang term referring to the tactical unit in a prison. Their duties include cell searches, drug raids, and breaking up riots; so called because, in their protective padding and helmets, they resemble the Teenage Mutant Ninja Turtles.

Gladiator school is a medium to maximum security prison where fighting is much more common.

That's a mean little bullet right there.

Yes. He's been schooled at Cimarron down in Tucson.

HANDBALL PLAYING ONLY

DNH stands for "do not house," an official designation signifying that two prisoners cannot be housed on the same yard because they are enemies.

How come you never been shipped to the florence complex?

I got a DNH there; my brother's murderer.

Zoo-zoos and wham-whams are snacks bought from the commissary and are often used to pay off debts.

STORE LIST

10 Candy Bars	6.00
10 Sodas	6.00
4 Bags Nachos	3.40
6 Cans Tuna	6.40
2 Hot Sauce	3.60
6 Vienna Sausage	4.80
	$30.20
= 1 Paper of Heroin	

Staying clean is getting easier. I still go to bars that have live music.

And all my new friends are musicians...

...as well as some old ones.

OPEN-MIKE NITE at
RULA BULA
FEATURING
WALT RICHARDSON

We met at Tony's Native New Yorker back in 1983. Tony's was in Tempe and featured many of Arizona's best bands, Walt not the least.

Tony's
Native New Yorker
This Month
WALT RICHARDSON
SMALL PAUL
HANS OLSON
CHUCK HALL

Walt was—and still is—the unofficial mayor of Tempe...

...and is the only friend I have left from before my being released from Prison in March 2002.

What about friends from Connecticut? Or all those guys you did time with?

I didn't have many friends back east and had even less in Prison.

Walt once Played at the Federal Correctional Institution, Phoenix, the Prison I called home from 1988 to 1989.

I was doing two years for counterfeiting...

Sentencing Transcript
Matthew Parker
DOB 04/05/1960
POB Bpt., CT
BOP No. 19972-008
FBI No. 548904CA5

Arrested or received
11/11/1987 probation
violation, dealing in
counterfeit obligations
Probation revoked
Sentence 2Y confinement

...when I spotted the flyer outside my cell.

Appearing Live
Walt Richardson
and The Morning
Star Band
Saturday
on
the Rec Yard

He performed on the basket-ball court. Walt is a master of reggae, but he also plays folk and rhythm and blues.

I wasn't allowed to talk to him when he played at the prison, but it was good to see him again...

...and to hear him.

I run into Walt again when I'm in school at SCC.

Long time, Walt. How've you been?

Too blessed to be stressed.

He is MC at the McDowell Mountain Music Festival. We're filming it for MCTV, the college station where I work.

THE McDOWELL MOUNTAIN MUSIC FESTIVAL
APRIL 21-24, 2004
WESTWORLD POLO GROUNDS
SCOTTSDALE

It's good to see him again..

And to hear him.

I meet Billy Cioffi at SCC in 2002.

I've witnessed too much, so I need protection.

Billy explains to me that he's invented his own kind of witness protection program.

Just about everybody over 40 in this fuckin' city is witness protection. They just don't realize it.

STUDEN

It's why he moved to Scottsdale after 25 years in Hollywood.

People like me and you, Matthew, are self-marginalized.

I understood his cocnept of self-marginalization but wondered how we fit into the literary theory of Other.

That's easy. Everybody wants to be some-place else.

That's someplace else.

Not me. I just wanted to be high all the time.

He's been a musician all his life and has played with the likes of Bo Diddley, Del Shannon, Chuck Berry, and Leslie Gore.

He's also an ex junkie.

There are lots of ex junkies in the county.

MARICOPA COUNTY COMMUNITY COLLEGE

MARICOPA COUNTY JAIL

And lots of expert survivors.

STUDY ABROAD

Like me, Billy has returned to school.

ADULT RE-ENTRIES

His mother wanted him to go to college and study law.

Go to college, Billy. Shape your destiny.

And my mom wanted the same for me.

Become a lawyer, Matthew, and support me in my old age.

Billy's mom envisioned him as a lawyer, judge, politician, or even governor of New York.

BILLY AMBULANCE CHASERS

BILLY for STATE SENATE

My mom just wanted me to get an education.

A college degree is your way out of this life of poverty and crime.

Yes. I can learn how to steal legally.

Billy's mother never forgave him for spurning her plans for him.

I turn my back on black sheep.

When I quit high school, my mom forgave me in a week.

It's your choice. Hope you like working for a living.

Every one of Billy's five siblings is a college graduate.

No one in my family except my sister went to college.

Billy and I are both in the process of trying to make things right.

It's not that I need a college degree to survive...

...but more that I feel naked without it.

We become close after taking an arts and humanities class with Sandy, the professor who sent me to New York in the fall of 2003.

Who can equate Frankenstein with Prometheus?

gothic horror romantic

Baroque rococo

After class we often discuss politics.

You can't have an egalitarian society if you deny citizens basic human rights.

Yes. The great red flaw. Not exactly what Marx had in mind.

As the election of 2004 approaches, Billy and I argue over who will win.

Kerry can't lose.

Glad you think so.

Billy is not so certain of Kerry's success. As evidence of this, he quotes H. L. Mencken verbatim.

Why so negative?

No one has ever gone broke underestimating the intelligence of the American public.

I laugh at this, assured of Kerry's victory.

Ha ha ha ha. You're a funny guy. Why do you think Bush will win reelection?

Because there are only two kinds of people in the world...

Then I get angry, because he might be right.

...scared white men and everybody else.

My dream of attending Columbia is still nested nicely in my brain.

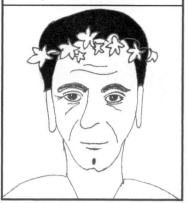

In May of 2004 my boss at MCTV gets a call from administration.

The dean of students wants to see Matthew Parker.

I'm thinking that they want to see me because I'm such a good student...

Your good grades reflect your commitment to rehabilitation, so...

...and that they're going to give me an award.

...We'd like to honor you with this award.

SQUARE ROOT FOUNDATION

$1,000 Scholarship

Awarded to:

Matthew Parker

for Studiously Rehabilitating His Self

When I arrive, the dean of students is there along with some guy who has a badge clipped to his belt.

SECURITY CAMPUS POLICE 6969

I start sweating, thinking they'd dredged up some obscure crime from my past.

Fuck. What could it be? Shoplifting? Counterfeiting? Ice fishing without a license?

But they tell me I'm under investigation for sexual harassment.

Seems you met a girl here on campus and sent her some lewd emails?

I'm furious...

You scared the shit out of me for that?

...and in no mood to be interrogated.

So did you in fact send the emails?

Of course I did. I've been in prison for a quarter of my life.

Here's what happened. I met a girl, probably in her early thirties, on campus, and we went out to lunch.

So, tell me about yourself.

There seemed to be a spark, but when I told her about my past, she retreated.

I was a junkie for most of my adult life and have been to prison five times.

I emailed her, telling her I not only wanted but actually needed to get laid, and that it would be really nice if it was her.

She responded by retreating further, and I responded with insults.

WAHOO MAIL

MAIL | CONTACTS | CALENDAR | NOTEP

Send | Save as Draft | Cancel

To:
Cc:
ject:

Attach File

Dear Girl,
Even a polite "fuck off" is preferable to blatant indifference, but then, callousness is as rampant as classlessness.

She was afraid of me because of my criminal record, but she told them she didn't want me to get in any trouble.

We're glad you came to us with this.

Of course not.

Me, too. But you're not gonna kick him out of school, are you?

I send a letter to the SCC administrators and basically tell them to fuck off. Not the most constructive move. They respond with a letter of their own:

Dean of Student Services
Sentencing and disposition of Student Matthew Parker—
Suspension from all classes and employment and barred from SCC campus for a period of six months, after which time Mr. Parker may resume his employment at MCTV. Probation for one year, after which time this matter can be set aside.

This includes the summer math class I was taking so I could reapply to Columbia in the fall. My Ivy League dreams are torched.

I've lost my chance to transfer to one of the few fed joints of higher learning.

CLUB FED

So I have to do my time in a state joint: Arizona State, to be exact, but at least I'm out of that fucking county.

ASU

To help me recover, I go to the Eric Clapton Cross-roads Guitar Festival.

It's held in the Cotton Bowl in Dallas, June 2004.

And the lineup is phenomenal.

Eric Clapton, Jeff Beck, Ron Block, Booker T and the MGs, JJ Cale, Larry Carlton, Robert Cray, Bo Diddley, Jerry Douglas, Vince Gill, Buddy Guy, David Hidalgo, Eric Johnson, BB King, Sonny Landreth, Jonny Lang, John Mayer, Pat Metheny, Robert Randolph, Duke Robillard, Carlos Santana, Hubert Sumlin, James Taylor, Steve Vai, Joe Walsh, and ZZ Top.

A friend and I sit under the hot Texas sun and enjoy the music...

...which goes on well into the night.

We walk out on ZZ Top, the final act, when they start playing that 1980s MTV crap.

Let's go.

No shit.

I guess no one told them it's a blues festival.

A month or so after the concert, Mom and I drive her Mustang up to Idaho and rescue my cousin Marcia...

...and her four daughters:

Deana

Alison

Stephanie

Nina

Each girl has a different father, all from Bridgeport.

Marcia is my first cousin, daughter of my mom's younger sister, Barbara, who died in 1984.

Your aunt Barbara died.

Heart attack.

What? How?

She drifted for a time, stayed in Arizona in the late 1990s, then got dumped in Idaho by a guy I did time with.

Coeur d'Alene

We move them into our four bedroom house, and our quiet lives suddenly become very hectic. I have to build an addition to accomodate all these newfound cousins.

I abruptly go from living with thousands of men in crowded prisons to sharing a small home with six women.

Well, two women and four girls.

Like prison, it's hard to get a spot in the bathroom.

You just wait your turn, buddy.

It's also about this time that I start dating a girl from New Jersey.

We met at one of the hottest clubs in Phoenix.

♫ Rhythm Room
Phoenix's Roots + Blues club

She meets all my friends from the funk band Knee-deep but then shocks me after I take her to Chez Nous, another Phoenix club that features funky music.

That was a nigger bar you took me to.

I lecture her on the evils of racism and think I've made her understand.

Listen. I was locked up with enough Nazi racist bastards in prison that I really don't want to spend my time fucking one.

G ♥ AZ

But I let her go when she tells me, just a few nights later, that she doesn't believe in evolution.

I'm not descended from no monkey.

PRIMATES
BAR AND GRILL

67

I'm accepted into Barrett, the Honors College, at Arizona State University.

A small compensation, kind of like being a trustee in prison.

Trustees have earned a position of trust, or honor, by being on their best behavior.

HONOR DORM

I guess you can say that I've been on my best behavior.

Are you staring at our tits?

We stand corrected.

Who? Me? Of course not. Just because I have a penis doesn't mean I have to acknowledge its functionality. That would be admitting to a form of biological determinism.

ARIZONA STATE UNIVERSITY

Barrett doesn't ask about prior possession charges...

ASU BARRETT
The Honors College
ARIZONA STATE UNIVERSITY

Imaginary Application Form for Prospective Honorees

Transfer Students
1.) GPA
2.) Statement of Purpose

Note No. 1: Past criminal history, even unspeakably heinous possession of narcotics charges, carries no weight with this body.

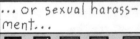

...or sexual harassment...

Are you staring at my tits?

Yes.

...or fantasies of kidnapping.

ASU BARRETT
The Honors College
ARIZONA STATE UNIVERSITY

Note No. 2: Please keep all fancies of the kidnapping and subsequent holding (for whatever purpose) of any and all neocons to yourself. Barrett recognizes the right to hold such fantasies dear but has no wish to disseminate them. Instead, we suggest you write your honors thesis on them.

Which is a good thing.

ASU BARRETT
The Honors College
ARIZONA STATE UNIVERSITY

Final Disclaimer:

In closing, we at Barrett would like to add that we just about give a python's penis what you've done in the past, whose tits you are looking at now, or what your fantasies for the future might be.

I'm starting to figure out that prisons and universities are similar.

Both are run by bureaucrats.

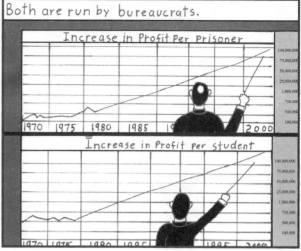

Increase in Profit Per Prisoner

Increase in Profit Per Student

I went from a prison yard to a college campus.

From muscular men to women with fake tits.

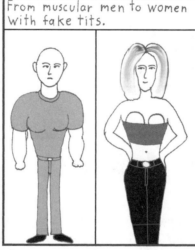

And cell phones.

YOU BOOBS

There are lots of fake tits and cell phones at Arizona State.

Where are you?

No. Where are you?

No. Where are you?

It's a wonder that they haven't yet combined the two.

Hello?

There were no tits in prison, but lots of pecs.

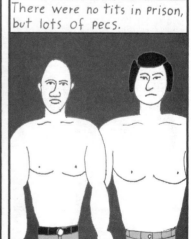

Lots of large pecs on lots of macho men. Some even had Nazi symbols tattooed on their pecs...

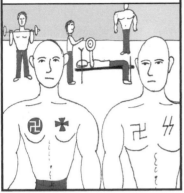

... and on other parts of their bodies.

Self-preservation prevented me from pointing out the obvious to them:

Had Hitler succeeded, you'd be in line behind the gypsies.

Instead I kept my mouth shut...

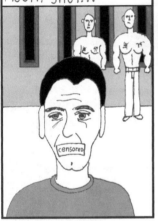

censored

...and mourned my tit-less existence.

No tits, no drugs, no wine, no women,..

But there is no shortage of tits at Arizona State...

...though the tits do me no good, since none of the scantily clad girls here are allowing me to touch theirs.

Look, but don't touch.

Even the girls with fake ones.

Really look, but don't touch.

One of my problems is that I think that every girl who smiles at me or is nice to me...

Hi there.

Hello.

... wants to fuck me.

Take me now.

I'm wrong, of course.

Well, you're a really nice guy, and...

But I can't see it, which is what had gotten me kicked out of Scottsdale Community College.

She wants me. I know she does. I'll just send her a dirty email to make sure.

I wonder at what point I'll cross into the dirty-old-man stage.

Young and horny.

Old and Perverted.

If indeed I haven't already.

Dirty Old Man
Application Form

To qualify for dirty-old-man status, you must meet the following requirements:

1.) Be over the age of 40
2.) Have at least one accusation of sexual harassment.
3.) Sing along to Viagra commercials.

I have a rule about women.

RULES TO FUCK BY

Never talk to women under 30.

How old are you?

It seems a sensible rule, as women appear to be slightly crazy until they reach that magical age.

I want the bosom of the earth returned to the navel of the feminine while drinking the violence of sex with your eyes only.

THE MARCH OF THE SILICON SOLDIERS

But I may follow this rule simply because women under 30 won't fuck me anymore.

Hi.

Filthy old pervert.

I never was much good at picking up women...

...although, on occasion, they had little trouble picking me up.

Until they found out I was an ex con and an ex junkie.

They then had little or no trouble dumping me.

At Arizona State, this isn't a problem, as none of them will date me to begin with. Not even the feminists.

Although feminist theory, with the main focus on equal rights for all, seemed to preclude this.

In theory.

72

As an English major, I'm learning all about theory.

What is literature?
Why should we care?
Authors's intent?
What's writ[?]

Modernism
Chemical and mechanized warfare
Conrad   Kafka
Proust   Yeats

There are the Modernists...

STREAM OF CONSCIOUSNESS

Joyce

Woolf

...the Realists...

You can't go back to anything.

W. D. HOWELLS

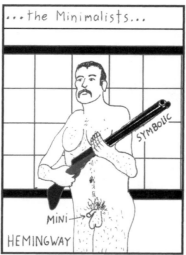

...the Minimalists...

SYMBOLIC

Mini

HEMINGWAY

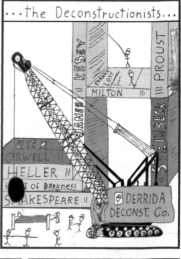

...the Deconstructionists...

KESEY
PROUST
HENRY JOYCE
MILTON
JAMES
STEINBECK
ORWELL
HELLER
HEART of DARKNESS
SHAKESPEARE
DERRIDA DECONST. Co.

...the Post-Structuralists...

Signifier   Signified

No truth.   No shit?

Siamese Sins

...and, of course, the Post modernists.

Nothing definite exists. Not even irony.

HEIDEGGER

To name a few.

PRAGMATISM

FORMALISM

HISTORICISM

POST-COLONIALISM

AESTHETICISM

AD NAUSEAMISM

But doing time with literary theorists is much easier than doing time with white supremacists.

There'll be a race riot on the ball field after chow. Bring your shanks.

For one thing, literary theorists are much less violent.

There'll be a reading on race relations in the student center after class. Bring your Shakespeare.

Revenge
Tragedy
Titus
Othello
Cleopatr

Nor are all their movements totally alien to me.

Most junkies are nihilists with their destructive bent turned inward.

Michel Foucault's theory of Pan-opticon describes the Madison Street Jail perfectly.

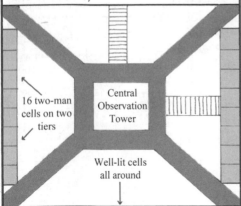

16 two-man cells on two tiers

Central Observation Tower

Well-lit cells all around

But Foucault took his theory a step further by describing modern society as a Panopticon.

Our society is one not of spectacle but of surveillance.

Modern society strives, according to Foucault, to exert a subtle yet powerful control over its citizens by making those citizens unwitting controllers seated firmly in the central tower.

He who is subjected to a field of visibility, and who knows it, assumes responsibility for the constraints of power.

Sounds like Facebook to me.

74

Chapter 4

My brother John was murdered in February of 1980.

≡ The Phoenix Deserter
February 3, 1980

Convicted Rapist Arrested for South Mountain Murder

By Gunther Gladstone

Francis Thomas, a convicted rapist who was just released early on parole from San Quentin prison in California, was arrested yesterday in Oklahoma for the stabbing death of Harold John Parker.

Parker's body was found in the South Mountain Recreat[ion] area by Phoenix police. After follo[w] up on local leads, the police got a break when a hitchhiker from T[ ] called and told the[ ]

Purportedly for eight bucks.

What was his motive?

Robbery.

Although the murderer claimed John was a snitch.

Have you anything to say before sentencing?

I killed him 'cause he was a rat, yer honor.

Much later, I'd learn in prison that you can't call somebody a snitch without solid proof, preferably paperwork from a court.

Superior Court of California
County of Los Angeles

Defendant Heidi Fleiss was convicted of solicitation of prostitution on the direct testimony in open court of that rat Charlie Sheen, who was granted immunity on some very minor crimes in exchange for his testimony.

It would be too easy to destroy an enemy by accusing him of being a rat, or worse.

That guy's a snitch rapist cho mo.

But since John's murderer was a convicted rapist, he already fell into the worse category.

What're we gonna do about Freddie the rapist?

Kill him?

Extort him. What else?

Naw. Not when he can pay up.

I knew he was being extorted because, over the years and through the prisons, I'd met guys who knew him.

Yeah, I remember him from South Unit. We called him Heart Attack Fred 'cause he was always faking like he was dying.

I missed John's funeral. My excuse was that I was too strung out to make the trip to Arizona.

You're not coming out for the funeral?

You gonna be all right?

No. Can't miss work. I'll send Diane and the baby instead.

I'll be fine.

This may or may not have been true, but I was certainly doing a lot of heroin at the time.

Soon after John died, I split up with Diane and became homeless.

Gotta go, baby.

I know. I'm surprised you haven't left sooner.

This left my son fatherless, although I didn't think so at the time because I'd take him on the occasional Sunday.

Beardsley Zoological Gardens

I sort of took John's place in the family, wandering the streets from high to high.

Alms for the sober?

The only difference was that I worked. For a time.

I slept in the park at night but still made it to work at the tool and die shop every day.

You got grass in your hair.

Thanks.

Finally a kindly girl took me in and let me sleep on the couch in her living room.

She would sometimes sneak out of her bedroom in the dead of night and fuck the shit out of me.

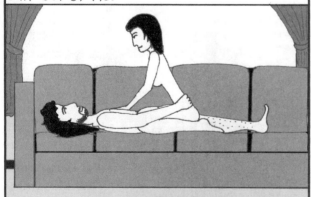

I didn't have any problems finding girls who wanted to fuck me in those days.

76

I serve my six months of probation for sexual harassment at Scottsdale Community College and get my job back at MCTV in January of 2005.

Welcome back.

Thanks.

But they fire me again a week later by sending an email to my boss.

Subject: Mathew Parker
From: Sharon ████████
Date: Tue, 1 Feb 2005
To: James ████████

The SCC administration has determined that Matthew Parker is not a good fit for our orginization. You will have to inform him that his services are no longer needed. I will inform ████████ ████ to remove his key code by 5:00pm Wednesday and ████ will cancel his RPS effective the same time. Call me if you have any questions.

When my boss does call, they give a standard "we are cutting back" reason as to why they fired me...

They claim to be over budget.

...but no one believes this. It seems to me that they're suspicious of ex cons who need to get laid.

It's patently obvious that this man has every intention of using his penis.

I see that. Better fire him first.

As if there's any other kind of ex con.

I miss sex and food most of all. You?

Penny loafers and the ballet.

I pace the campus in fury, but no one will talk to me.

Nothing I can do.

Can't help you.

Sorry.

Get lost.

So I go to the Maricopa Community Colleges Governing Board meeting, a monthly event filmed by MCTV.

And launch into a tirade in front of all those stuffy bureaucrats.

I was assured that I'd be able to return to my job at MCTV.

They're embarrassed by me. I can see in their faces that they wish I'd just go away.

77

Soon after the board meeting Billy and I go to see Walt Richardson at an Irish pub in Tempe.

Walt holds an open-mike night there every Tuesday.

RÚLA BÚLA SADDLERY

On this particular night, Walt has a message for me.

I met a sort of friend of yours last night.

He'd run into Jerry Walker, one of the Maricopa Community Colleges Governing Board members, at a gig he was playing at Gilbert Community College.

Jerry Walker is the resident homophobic Christian Southern values governing board member.

Beware of the man with the American flag tie.

They got to talking, my name came up, and he gave Walt his card to give to me.

So you know Mr. Parker?

Sure do.

Well, I want to help him.

Apparently Jerry is the only administrator who is on my side.

Community colleges are for the community, and we should help this man.

I call him and we set up a meeting on the Arizona State campus for when I'm between classes.

I don't care what you do so long as you ain't fooling around with no boys.

I met my best friend, Pete, in Spanish class in 1975, when I was a freshman at Central High School.

What are you doing?

Holy shit.

Rolling a joint.

He ended up graduating. I didn't.

I, in fact, quit school the following April.

I just can't take all the fucking rules.

It's your choice, but you're making a mistake.

Still, we became very close.

Come on. I'll drive you home.

Cool.

He had a car and I had a closet full of marijuana.

Drive me to my weed.

We're on our way.

Pete was with me the night I first stuck a needle in my arm.

What're you doing?

Experimenting.

And was angry at me for doing so.

You're a fucking idiot.

I know.

I was 16 at the time, and as cool as my family was, Pete knew that this would have really pissed them off.

Happy Birthday Matthew

79

Pete was also there for me when John was murdered in February of 1980.

Matthew, I just heard. Are you all right?

I'll be right over.

Yeah. Ok.

He picked me up and drove me around for hours.

Want another one?

Sure.

We drank beer and smoked weed while cruising through the woods of Connecticut.

Pretty country.

Yes.

After graduating from high school, Pete took a job in a gas station as a mechanic.

I went back to a different high school in the fall of 1976 and quit again the following April.

HARDING HIGH SCHOOL

My last attempt to finish school was at Cranberry High in the woods of Pennsylvania in the fall of 1977.

EDUCATION DR.

It was after returning to Bridgeport from Pennsylvania in January of 1978 that I took the job at Mohawk Tool & Die.

We make injection molds here. Are you familiar with them?

No.

The gas station where Pete worked was close to Mohawk and on my way up to the park where I lived homeless after John died.

Beardsley Park

Pete's gas station

Mohawk Tool & Die

Noble Av.

North Av.

Boston Av.

East Main St.

Main St.

Capitol Av.

Madison Av.

Park Av.

2000 ft.

Every night I'd get off at five and meet up with Pete at his job.

Hey, bud, you ready to go?

In a minute. Just let me get this engine timed.

In September of 1980, Pete and I and another friend went camping.

I hated camping. Anyone who's been homeless recognizes camping as just more of the same.

Nothing like a fresh meal cooked over an open fire.

And good wine.

But I needed to get my head on straight and try to kick heroin, and Pete offered to help in the only way he knew how.

A few days in the woods will do you good.

Blah.

To Pete, any problem, even heroin addiction, could be solved with a trip back to nature lubed with large amounts of alcohol.

VACANCY

BYOB

For him, nothing was more healing than beer and nature.

Here, have another beer.

RALPH

Godliness for Pete was shitting in the woods.

Although sick most of the time, I avoided the worst pangs of withdrawal by getting, and staying, drunk.

He looks a little better today.

Yes.

RALPH

We left on a Sunday night.

81

The next day, I was walking home from work, intending to stop by to see Pete as usual.

Pete's car wasn't at the gas station, so I asked another mechanic where he was.

Hey, Phil. Where's Pete? Did he call in sick?

Oh, hey, Matt. How you doing?

He seemed scared at first and wouldn't answer me.

I'm fine. Where's Pete?

You haven't heard?

Heard what?

He walked into the office then and handed me the local paper.

Partly Cloudy, high of 73

The Bridgeport Post

Horoscope comics movies

Monday, September 15, 1980

Fireman's son dies in shooting

I think I was in a mild state of shock.

Phil, lend me me ten bucks.

What?

Give me ten bucks, mother fucker.

Pete was killed by his friend Chas, who claimed the shooting was an accident.

He tried to take the gun from me and it went off.

I didn't know, and still don't know, if this was true or not.

Certainly Pete's parents believed that it was no accident.

He's lying.

Yes.

That night, I walked the rest of the way up to Beardsley Park in a daze, stopping only to buy a six-pack with Phil's $10.

Can I help you?

CAN I HELP YOU?

What?

Oh. Yes. A six-pack of Bud.

You M Be 18 OLD

At the Park, everyone was partying, so I went off and sat by myself.

Hey, Matt. Want some acid?

NO.

A woman I knew vaguely as Maria came over to offer condolences.

I'm sorry about your friend, although I didn't know him.

I handed her a beer and she sat down next to me. She was amazingly pretty. We did not speak.

It was odd sitting there, because I was suddenly torn between intense grief and infinite desire.

I felt guilty about this.

I didn't think the two emotions belonged together.

Maria taught me otherwise.

You have a boyfriend? Get rid of him.

Yes. Ok.

83

She ended up being the first woman I ever loved.

And the last one, for a long, long time.

She took Pete's place, in that she was the one I now met every night after work.

And throughout his wake and funeral she barely left my side.

Except at night, because, being only 17 and, typically, always in trouble, she had an 8:30 curfew.

Good night.

Good night.

See you tomorrow?

Of course. Same place.

About a month after we met she ran away and even quit high school to be with me.

You sure you don't mind me dropping out?

I'd rather you didn't, but who the fuck am I to lecture anyone on education?

We rented an apartment from some Hell's Angels on the East Side of Bridgeport.

I love you.

Oh yeah? Well I love my fucking rent.

FTM

Maria and I were making love when we heard on the radio that John Lennon had been murdered.

John Lennon IS dead.

It was Maria, along with her friend Spacey Tracy, whom I took to Central Park the following Sunday.

95

Except for Maria, 1980 was a very bad year.

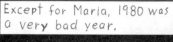

Tic tac toe, three murders in a row.

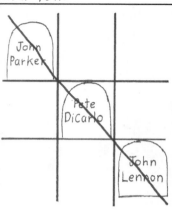

John Parker

Pete DiCarlo

John Lennon

I was absolutely crazy about Maria.

But I was crazy for narcotics first...

I love heroin.

I love acid, and ludes, and whiskey...

...and would step on those who got in the way of my trying to obtain them.

Especially those I was crazy for.

I thought you were taking me out?

Nope. Gotta go cop.

And all that violent death gave me the excuse I needed to get strung out again.

You're doing too much heroin.

I need it. I can't cope.

Well, I can't cope either.

Then have a fucking beer.

I knew it was only a matter of time until Maria would be strung out, as well.

Beer don't work.

Nope.

Barbiturates then?

Fuck.

I tried to discourage her from using...

This isn't a game, you know. Once you try it, there's no going back.

...but after bugging me constantly for months she began to wear me down.

I mean, Elvis was a junkie. That's pretty good company, no?

There are two main rules to being a junkie.

Rules to Shoot Dope By

Danger!
Do not open until strung out

The first is obvious: never get high alone, so you'll have someone else present if an overdose occurs.

Death Valley National Park

Unlike when you take too many pills, when you shoot too much heroin, you know immediately that it's too much.

Death Valley National Park

If you're alone, you may not be able to crawl your dying ass into a cold shower.

Ice-cold water on naked skin can shock you back to life.

The second rule is to never shoot someone up for the first time. You never forget the first person who shot you up and will often blame that person for the nightmare that follows.

It's all your fault.

Eviction Notice

And one good blast to the mainline will instantly dispel any fears of needles the first-timer may have had.

I thought you were afraid of needles?

Me? Afraid?

I was never very good with rules.

Rules to Be Conditioned By

Ivan Pavlov

WARNING!
Extremely Fragile

86

I lost my tool and die job a few months after meeting Maria, in November of 1980.

Mohawk Tool & Die
Pink Slip

Apprentice Matthew Parker is hereby terminated from further employment for being high all the time. We've put up with his fucking up for close to two years and we just can't take it anymore.

President, Mohawk Tool & Die

But I had learned to live out on the streets. Most of my childhood had been preparation for it.

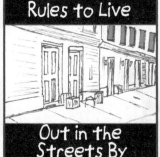

Rules to Live

Out in the Streets By

Every day was a struggle to come up with dope money. Paying rent and bills were secondary.

Where's my fucking rent?

After about a year and a half, the heroin tore Maria and me apart.

I can't say I didn't see it coming.

We're doing too much heroin. We can't keep this up.

If I had really loved her, I'd have stopped us both from using.

We are going to stop shooting heroin. Today.

But my love of heroin was stronger than my love of her.

Tomorrow. We're gonna kick tomorrow.

Cool.

Not that Maria was totally innocent. She wasn't. Before we ever got together she'd indulged in most of the hard drugs of the day except heroin.

Amphetamines

THC/PCP

LSD

Barbiturates   Cocaine

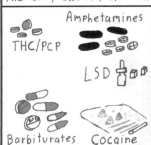

But I was the one who first shot her up.

Hold still. Not for long.

Sorry. I hate needles.

After being evicted from our second apartment, Maria returned home and I returned to the streets.

But I didn't last long out there. I eventually packed my meager belongings and ran away.

95 WEST
FORT
LEE

I wasn't just running away from Maria, but also from heroin...

...and Bridgeport...

...and homelessness...

...and joblessness...

CRANK
CONSTRUCTION
NOW HIRING!
HOMELESS
JUNKIES
NEED NOT
APPLY!

...and finally hoplessness.

EXISTENTIAL
EXCAVATION
NO
MEANINGFUL
WORK
AVAILABLE

I was running away to Arizona and, at the same time...

GLOBE 47
SUPERIOR 71
PHOENIX 139

...home to my mommy.

Hi, Mom.

You look like shit.

From my perspective, Jerry Walker has no pull among all those liberals at Scottsdale Community College in the winter of 2005.

We're trying to get you your job back.

I learn that I was fired by a woman who I never even met.

Well, you were fired by one of our deans, and...

I don't even know what she is the dean of, only that she is in a position of power over MCTV.

It's just a work-study job, and...

For reasons that no one can satisfactorily articulate, none of the administrators are coming to my rescue. The liberals have abandoned me, and so has, after a time, Jerry Walker.

We're doing what we can.

Bye.

It seems my pathetic work-study job has become a bone of contention between the two camps.

He deserves a second chance.

We can fire who we want.

One side acting supportive toward their token ex con while shanking me in the back...

Oh, I see you made the dean's list.

...and the other more tolerant of my past because they despise liberals in general...

Fucking liberals.

DO NOT TOUCH

...and political correctness in particular.

I'm working my way through college.

TABLE DANCES $20

Fucking academics.

This becomes a recurring theme throughout my journey into the realm of higher education.

We believe in rehabilitation.

Well, we'd love to hire you, but...

Meanwhile I become good friends with Ed, the lead guitarist and co-founder of the funk band Kneedeep. We begin going to conerts almost immediately.

Jeff Beck and BB King.

David Bowie with Macy Gray.

Steely Dan.

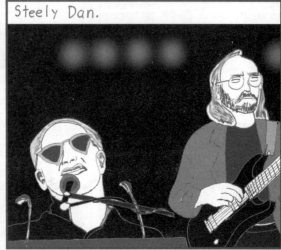

Mountain.

Dave Mason.

Leon Russell.

The Tubes.

Santana.

Prince with Lenny Kravitz.

Jethro Tull.

And, my all-time favorite, Roger Waters.

Ed also lends me an acoustic guitar, and I use it to channel off stress.

Hang on to this for as long as you need to.

Thanks.

Don't you have a paper due?

Later.

But it's Billy who shows me how to play it.

No. The F chord.

I also become close to Alex, the sax player of Kneedeep.

And the lead singer, Chris.

I do a portrait in pen and ink for Ed and give it to him on his birthday.

I also draw a detailed saxophone for Alex's **fiftieth**.

I'm almost done with a portrait of Sly Stone for Chris when I smear it with ink, ruining it.

These pieces of art take a long time to create—months in fact.

When asked why I give away my art, I explain that it's out of friendship.

There's a ton of work in that Hendrix portrait.

And it's a lot of work you put into your music.

And also out of gratitude.

But my music can be shared by many.

So can my art.

But fewer will see it.

Depends where you hang it.

PHAT LOVE

I credit the live music of Kneedeep for keeping me off heroin and out of prison.

True. But it still seems unfair.

Art begets art.

That rush you get from music you really love is the same as a heroin rush, only not as intense or prolonged.

The Kneedeep Experience gave me a place to be on weekends. Something to look forward to beyond my loneliness, even if it was just a dive bar.

Another beer?

No thanks. The music is enough.

Being an excellent student also makes it easier to stay clean.

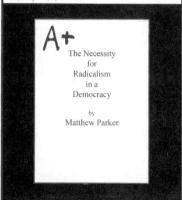

A+

The Necessity
for
Radicalism
in a
Democracy

by

Matthew Parker

I now channel my compulsion into more productive activites.

Compared to the hard work involved in being a junkie, becoming an honor student is ridiculously easy.

Chapter 5

What's wonderful about heroin is its anesthetizing qualities.

Heroin (diacetylmorphine); a powerful analgesic derived from morphine; first synthesized in England in 1874, but did not find wide use until it was resynthesized in Germany in 1897.

Etymology: originates from the German "heroisch," which signifies heroic; powerful; godlike.

While on it, you feel very little pain, either physical or mental.

How's your flu?

What flu?

Seconds after you shoot it into your vein you get a warm surge of pure joy, very much like that warm surge you get when hearing a favorite song.

Hey. I haven't heard this song in years. It reminds me of... never mind. Let's dance.

The rush only lasts for a few minutes, but the no-pain well-being continues for hours.

How you feeling now?

Like I just got fucked by Athena.

So being a junkie is much more than satisfying your addiction; it's the rush you're chasing.

So why do you always need more?

Because I want her to fuck me again.

Shooting cocaine offers a similar intense rush, but it's different, more edgy and teeth grinding, as if your favorite song's playing while you're speeding dangerously down the highway.

Like heroin, the cocaine rush only lasts for moments, at which point you crash hard; your song is over and you find yourself handcuffed in the back of a police car.

Why am I under arrest?

DUI and vehicular manslaughter.

The cocaine crash comes on quickly but is soon over; an hour or so of paranoid depression.

But...?

Relax. I was joking. You can go to sleep now.

Crashing from heroin, on the other hand, takes a long time to come on—24 hours from your last fix, but the effects can stretch on for days, even weeks.

The court orders your bond set at $5,000.

May as well be a million.

County jail was hard on me because I always had to kick heroin cold turkey.

Brrrr.

From 1986 until 2000, I probably kicked heroin 15 times in the Horseshoe.

W Washington St.

W Jefferson St.
Maricopa County Superior Court

S 4th Ave.

S 3rd Ave.

Madison St.

Madison Street Jail

S 1st Ave.

Jackson St.

S 2nd Ave.

The Horseshoe is what intake was called at the Madison Street Jail.

It's basically a large holding area in which inmates were processed, classified, and shipped out to any of a number of county jails.

Maricopa County Sheriff's Office
Parker, Matthew Joseph 04/05/1960
Booking Date: 12/29/1999

There were a series of cells side by side along three of four sides of a square. The fourth side was the courtroom.

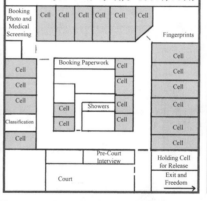

Booking Photo and Medical Screening | Cell | Cell | Cell | Cell | Cell | Cell
Fingerprints
Cell
Cell | Booking Paperwork | Cell | Cell
Cell | | | Cell
Cell | | | Cell
| Cell | Showers | Cell | Cell
Classification | | | Cell | Cell
Cell | Cell | | | Cell
| | Pre-Court Interview | Holding Cell for Release
| Court | | Exit and Freedom →

The first leg of the Horseshoe was for booking and prints...

...the second for pre-court and interview...

How many times have you been arrested?

I lost count.

...and the third was for classification, shower, and dress out.

Because of your priors you're classified as maximum security.

What else is new?

If I made it to the third leg I knew I wasn't getting out.

How much is your bond?

Five grand, Mom.

Are you crazy?

By this time I'd be in full withdrawal.

It often took 72 hours to get from booking to being shipped to one of a number of county jails spread like a pox over the desert landscape. More often than not, they'd keep me in Madison, in one of the 16 housing units on six floors of jail.

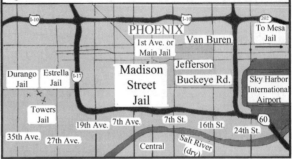

I would usually curl up on the concrete floor beneath a steel bunk and shiver in a cold sweat.

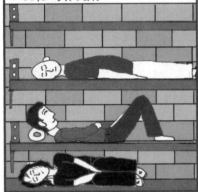

Heroin is basically artificial endorphins. Withdrawal makes you ill because of a lack of this chemical...

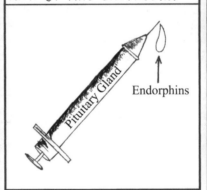

...and my brain would scream out a frantic SOS to my body:

Send up the endorphins. Send up the mother-fucking endorphins.

But my body was busy trying to keep all my cells from exploding outward and scattering my innards like shrapnel from a trillion microscopic grenades.

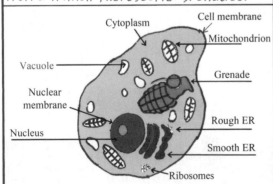

The Endorphin Bar and Grill had been shut down, its dark windows boarded up, its neon sign unplugged.

96

At this stage of withdrawal the body comes alive.

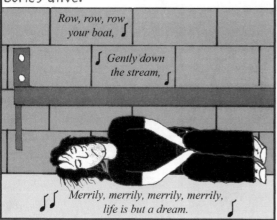

Row, row, row your boat, ♪

♪ *Gently down the stream,* ♪

♪♪ *Merrily, merrily, merrily, merrily, life is but a dream.* ♪

Nerve endings, loosed from their self-inflicted moorings, are suddenly in tune with what it means to be human.

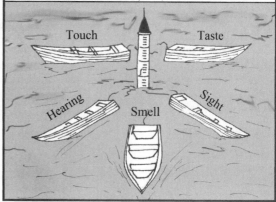

Touch Taste

Hearing Smell Sight

Touch is enhanced to a painful clarity.

The loins, shut down for so long, spontaneously pump semen.

Yuck.

Taste is metallic, highlighted with a tinge of rotting teeth.

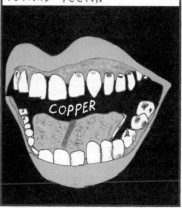

COPPER

Sight is blurred with seemingly endless burning tears impelled by a mass production of histamine.

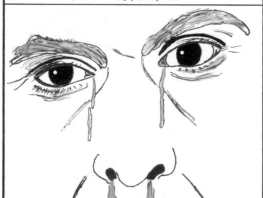

Hearing is abuzz with discordant voices and distant screams and slamming cell doors all humming a macabre opera.

And smell is assaulted with bad breath...

You don't look so good.

...unwashed bodies...

...funky feet...

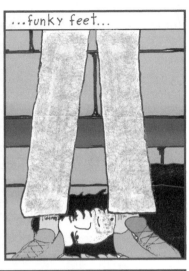

...sour milk and rotting fruit...

MILK

...and, overall, the amniotic stabbing of stale piss.

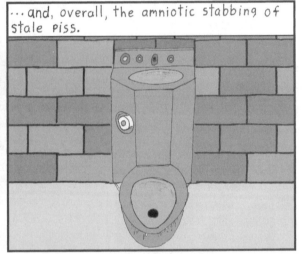

The mind, seeking refuge from the agony of the body, tries to retreat into sleep.

But the bugle has been blown, calling nerve endings to the assault.

They march from head to foot with bayonets poised.

Do you hear marching music?

The main cavalry rides to the guts.

MCSO

While foot soldiers spread to extremities.

The mind can only wander through the theater of the subconscious.

$E = mc^2$

My oblivion bubble has been burst.

THE LOTUS EATERS

Withdrawal is a painful reawakening of body and mind, but the worst of it is over in three days.

I once found Leo Tolstoy's "War and Peace" in the Horse-shoe, where books are not allowed.

I can't remember when this was, but I recall how thrilled I was to find it.

1990?
1991?
1992?
1994?
1995?
1996?
1998?
2000?

Good literature was rare in the county jail, and even rarer in the Horseshoe.

koontz
Zane Grey
Louis L'Amour
Stephen King
John Grisham
Sidney sheldon
Jackie Collins

Someone likely dumped it there when being trans-ferred to the Department of corrections.

You can't take that into DOC.

You Sure?

Positive.

I clung to it as if it were the rarest of treasures, which, in a very real sense, it was.

I inherited a love of Rus-sian literature from my aunt Barbara.

Is that a good book?

You bet your ass.

The Gulag Archipelago

She was one of my mom's younger sisters and my fav-orite aunt because she kept me knee deep in books since I was about five.

What's in that box?

More books from your auntie Barby.

By the time I found "War and Peace" I'd already read "Anna karenina," as well as a few of Tolstoy's short stories.

ANNA KARENINA

LEO TOLSTOY

I manged to keep "War and Peace" with me (and out of the view of the guards) for the time it took me to get a cell, after which I sa-vored every word.

PARKER.

In April of 1991, I found Aleksandr Solzhenitsyn's "The First Circle" in the housing area, or pod, of the Towers Jail.

There wasn't a library in the pods. Books just kind of floated around from cell to cell.

Who's got loose books?

I was familiar with Solzhenitsyn thanks to my aunt Barbara, particularly "Ivan Denisovich" and "The Gulag Archipelago."

Whatcha reading?

Russian what?

A book about Russian gulags.

The First Circle
Solzhenitsyn

But "The First Circle" was new to me.

Ahhh. It's based on Dante's first circle of Hell. Interesting.

Reading about the gulags always made me feel better about my own plight.

This place sucks.

Where?

Yeah, well, try doing hard labor in Siberia in winter.

In thinking about it now, I wonder why this book didn't have more of an effect on me.

This is a really good book.

I can't wait to get out and shoot some more heroin.

Solzhenitsyn had one passion: writing. And I had one passion: heroin.

It never occurred to me to compare his passion with mine—how his was lofty and worthwhile, while mine was low-down and even mean.

1970 Nobel Prize in Literature Awarded to Alexandr Solzhenitsyn	1991 Sentencing for Matthew Parker Two (2) Years in the Arizona Department of Corrections

I was in an Arizona state prison on 9/11 when the planes hit the towers.

They locked the prison down for a week or so, presumably to prevent us from taking over the yard.

Hey. Why don't we hijack some airplanes?

And do what with them?

Fly them into the guard towers.

We don't have any guard towers.

For a week they escorted us to meals and then back to our cells, where there was nothing to do but watch the endless news reports.

It wasn't long before they blamed me for 9/11.

The Arizona Minuteman
The Last Refuge of the Patriot

Junkies Responsible for 9/11
Sales of Afghan Heroin Funds al Qaeda   By Gunther Gladstone

It was American junkies, they said, buying their heroin from Afghanistan, who supported groups like the Taliban.

Thank you.

Go with Allah.

This was utter bullshit. All my heroin came from Mexico.

Thank you.

Vaya con Dios.

But even if it was true, a simple legalization would cut off the supply of illicit cash flowing into the coffers of terrorists.

They legalized it.

Allah be fucked!

Then heroin becomes a commodity, like coffee or cigarettes...

$3.42 per pack

COFFEE   Laudanum   Tussinex   Morphine   Der

$4.00 $7.00 $12.00 $9.00 $1

... or Ritalin.

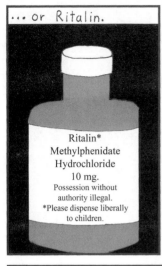

Ritalin*
Methylphenidate
Hydrochloride
10 mg.
Possession without
authority illegal.
*Please dispense liberally
to children.

Roughly eight grand is spent per year on each child attending a public school in America.

Average cost of public school student per year

$10,000				
$9,500				
$9,000				
$8,500				
$8,000				
$7,500				

2000 2001 2002 2003 2004 2

Not counting, of course, the Ritalin.

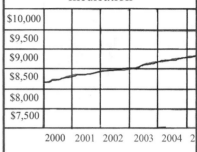

Average cost of public school student per year on medication

$10,000				
$9,500				
$9,000				
$8,500				
$8,000				
$7,500				

2000 2001 2002 2003 2004 2

By contrast, they spent about 30 grand a year to keep me locked up...

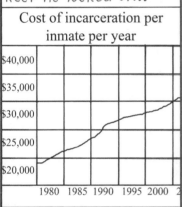

Cost of incarceration per inmate per year

$40,000				
$35,000				
$30,000				
$25,000				
$20,000				

1980 1985 1990 1995 2000 2

... not counting the heroin.

How much money do you think you've blown on heroin over the years?

Maybe a quarter million.

That's 330 grand over 11-odd years of incarceration.

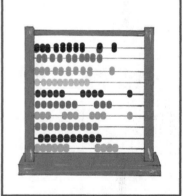

They could have sent me to Columbia.

I hereby sentence you to four years of hard Ivy.

As of June 30, 2003, Arizona state prisons housed 30,898 inmates.

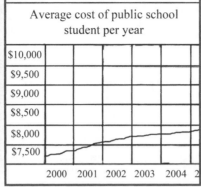

Increase in ADOC inmate population

	40,000
	35,000
	30,000
	25,000
	20,000
	15,000

1985 1990 1995 2000 2005

Of these, 4,430 (14.3 percent) had received their high school diplomas...

Not too many high school grads around here.

No. But we do have universal health care.

It took me seven days to hitchhike across the country in the summer of 1982, after Maria and I split up.

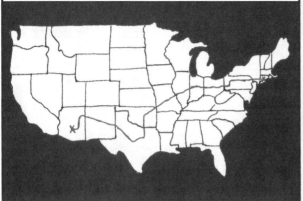

I had some money, so I stayed drunk the whole way.

SOUTH
79
Pittsburgh

And I did kick dope. Again.

Arizona was now my home, I figured. There was no returning to Bridgeport.

And I was determined, this time, to stay clean of heroin.

I took a maintenance job at a local mall, working the graveyard shift.

IDIAN
WELRY
SCOUNTS
OTIC
TS

USINESS
HOURS
:00 - 9:00
:00 - 10:00
LOSED

And replaced full-time heroin use with part-time alcohol abuse.

Hey, asshole. Wake up.

Maria was pissed off that I left.

How could you leave me here alone?

I told you I was going.

I didn't believe you.

No shit.

So after working and saving for a few months, I went back and got her.

105

Mom welcomed us both and got Maria a job as a maid at the hotel where she worked.

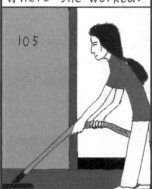

105

But my mom warned me that once a couple splits, there was no going back.

You can never return to the way it was.

And she was right. Maria and I tried to make it work, but we were drinking a lot and shooting cocaine on pay days.

Hold still, damn it.

Sorry.

To be clean held a different meaning to us. As long as we weren't shooting heroin we figured everything would be cool.

I had a tool and die job lined up and was waiting for it to come through.

Midland Precision Machining

Application for Employment
Name: Matthew Packer
DOB: 04/05/1968
Job Description: Apprentice tool maker
Past experience: Three years apprentice injection mold maker Mohawk Tool & Die

APPLICATION HOLD

In the interim, I worked in a local restaurant, first as a dishwasher, and then I was trained to be a short-order cook.

A yolk is broken.

By the time I rented us an apartment, Maria had started dating some guy she met at work.

Can I take you out?

Sure.

She suggested to me that we have an open relationship.

I think we should start seeing other people.

Ok. Now hold fucking still.

And I was just stupid enough to agree.

This is great. Now I can fuck other women.

106

At work, Maria didn't even try to hide the affair, and Mom was furious.

I'm going to kill that little bitch.

A week or so later, Maria moved in with him.

I'm leaving.

I handled it very badly: I whined like a cat in heat

Don't gooooooooo! Rooowwwwwnnnn!

I was no longer that rebel poet she fell in love with.

Good-bye pussy pussy pussy pussy.

ROWN.

But when the guy beat her up, she had no one left to crawl back to.

He punched me in the face—rooowwwnnn.

She was homesick and wanted to return to Bridgeport.

I wanna go home.

I told her that taking a bus cross country was dangerous.

Wait a week or two and I'll buy you a plane ticket.

But she told me she'd take the bus to Vegas, where she had rich relatives, and they'd buy her a plane ticket.

No. I'm going now.

She was with these relatives for a few days, and they put her on a cross-country bus.

Greycat Bus Line

107

Chapter 6

I'm still not having any luck with women by the time I begin my second semester at Arizona State University in 2005.

Hi.

So I try Internet dating in an effort to fill my loneliness. But I find that most of the women I meet are married and just want to have a fling.

Fuck me and go home.

Ok.

This is fine with me for a time. But after a while it starts to get old.

Are we hooking up later?

Not tonight. I have a heartache.

I still crave intimacy, and love.

Doesn't anyone just snuggle anymore?

The kind of love I had with Maria.

So I start looking abroad.

Find a Wife in Foreign Lands
Mail-order Brides from All over the World

Why put up with greedy American women? View our brochure of foreign ladies who want to meet American men today!

Ship to

Fragile
Handle with care

All of our girls are thoroughly inspected and 100% USDA approved. Find true love and loyalty. Order your full-color catalog right now!

Japan, China, Russia. I'm the virtual international playboy.

WAHOO MAIL

| Mail | Calendar | Contacts |

Send Cancel Save

Attach

Dear Chinese Girl,
I'm desperately lonely and recently bereft of occidental decadence. Looking for love and possibly marriage. I'm also an ex con and an ex junkie. Hope this doesn't change anything.

Russian girls are the most scandalous.

UNITED STATES

Department of State

Warning on Russian Bride Scams: Known as "Boris and Natasha" scams because Natasha usually turns out to be a Boris.

They will tell you they love you after a week of exchanged emails and ask for money after two.

WAHOO MAIL

| Mail | Calendar | Contacts |

Send Cancel Save

Attach

Dear Matthew,
I love you. Oh, by the way, the horse died on our farm and I need $400 for a new one.
Love,
Natasha

It's not long before I turn my eyes south, to Latinas.

°PHOENIX

Mujeres de Mexico Para Gringos: Hundreds of beautiful Mexican women looking for marriage and life partners.

South American brides. Exotic Latinas. Singles vacations, personal introductions, translators provided throughout South America. Meet your dark Latina bride today.

I email a girl from Peru and make plans to visit.

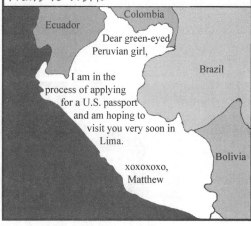

Colombia

Ecuador

Brazil

Dear green-eyed Peruvian girl,

I am in the process of applying for a U.S. passport and am hoping to visit you very soon in Lima.

xoxoxoxo, Matthew

Bolivia

But they deny me a passport.

UNITED STATES

Department of State
Passport Division

DS-11 Application form for a U.S. Passport. (You must submit this form in person at an acceptance facility or passport agency.)
Name: Matthew Parker
DOB: 04/05/1960
POB: Bridgeport, CT

APPLICATION DENIED

Not for my prior felonies, or even my refusal to pay my fines...

Maricopa County Superior Court

Dear Matthew Parker,
You owe us money. Lots of money.

Dear Maricopa County Superior Court,

Go take a flying fuck at a rolling doughnut.
Sincerely,
Matthew Parker

...but because of welfare fraud: Diane collecting welfare while we were married.

It's easy. Just tell them you don't know who the father is.

Basically I'm told that I owe back child support.

STATE OF CONNECTICUT
Department of Social Services
Child Support Division

Dear Matthew Parker,

Your passport application will continue to be denied until you pay your entire child support arrears. You cannot make payments on these arrears. They must be paid in full in order for you to obtain a U.S. passport.

They want me to pay roughly $8,000 to the State of Connecticut, which is almost the exact amount I owe the State of Arizona in fines.

STATE OF CONNECTICUT
Department of Social Services
Child Support Division

Matthew Parker
Child Support Arrears
Please pay this amount:
$8,789.63

STATE OF ARIZONA
County of Maricopa
Superior Court Division

Matthew Parker
Total Fines and Court Costs
Please pay this amount:
$8,621.00

Constitutionally speaking, they can't send you to prison and fine you.

I hereby sentence you to two years in the Arizona Department of corrections.

That's double jeopardy.

The Fifth Amendment*

No person shall be held to answer for a capital, or otherwise infamous crime, unless on a presentment or indictment of a Grand Jury...nor shall any person be subject for the same offense to be twice put in jeopardy of life or limb...

*Restitution does not fall under the double-jeopardy clause because it involves recompense to a victim.

What Arizona State will do is fine you anyway, then use your inability to pay your fines to withhold your civil rights.

And fine you 2,000 dollars plus court costs.

The equal protection clause of the XIV Amendment to the U.S. Constitution is not meant to ensure equality for poor people.

Sorry. If you can't pay your fines you can't vote.

But doesn't that favor the rich convicts?

Voter Registration

Is it?

The Fourteenth Amendment

No State shall make or enforce any law which shall abridge the privileges or immunities of citizens of the United States; nor shall any State deprive any person of life, liberty, or property, without due process of law; nor deny to any person within its jurisdiction the equal protection of the laws.

I fly the girl up from Peru.

Phoenix

Lima

She is incredibly beautiful, but lousy in bed, and mean.

You snore too loudly. I cannot sleep. You stay awake with me. Yes?

Yes.

And she makes me use a condom.

No puedes tocar mi concha sin condón.

Lo sé.

In the winter of 1983, soon after Maria and I broke up, I started dating Elaine. We met at Hobo Joe's, the diner where I worked as a cook.

You're dating Elaine!

Yep.

This way, please.

She broke up with me when she saw me shoot up.

Oh my God!

It wasn't even heroin, but some bathtub speed that my roommate, Davey, who was also a cook at Hobo Joe's, had whipped up in our kitchen.

A few Vicks inhalers. Some muriatic acid.

Some months later I asked my boss for a few days off to attend the US Festival in California, a huge, three-day rock concert put on by Steve Wozniak of Apple Computers.

I need four days off.

For what?

I want to go to this concert in California.

Forget it.

She refused, so I quit, walking right out the door during the breakfast rush.

Hey. Where you going?

Davey and I hitched a ride to the US Festival with another friend. It took place at Glen Helen Park in San Bernardino.

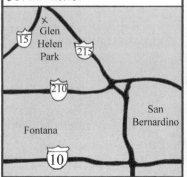

15 Glen Helen Park

215

210

Fontana

San Bernardino

10

We had very little money, so we slept in the car and planned on sneaking into the concert.

It's hot in here.

Go to sleep.

HOTEL

Air conditioned

The first day we snuck in easily.

"I put our tickets in this box." "Hurry UP." "Let's Go." "What's the hold-UP?"

Some of the bands were the Divinyls, INXS, Oingo Boingo, the English Beat, and Men at Work.

Including the Stray Cats...

...and the Clash.

The third-day lineup included Berlin.

U2.

Missing Persons.

The Pretenders.

Joe Walsh.

Stevie Nicks.

And David Bowie.

The second day was Heavy Metal day, and neither Davey nor I had any interest in that kind of music.

Dude. I just banged my head on the stage.

Awesome

SECURITY

113

We stayed in the parking lot and drank hot beer.

Upon our return to Scottsdale we lost our apartment for not paying our rent.

EVICTION

NOTICE

You are hereby ordered to vacate the premises

Maricopa County Sheriff's Office

This was an old trick. Pay first and last month's rent, then dodge the landlord until they have no choice but to initiate eviction proceedings, which took months.

Parker. Where's my rent?

Next week.

Also, that tool and die job I'd been waiting on for nine months was still on hold.

Sorry, but we are waiting on more orders to come in.

MITS
PRECIS
TOO

So I bought a bus ticket and an ounce of hash and returned to Bridgeport, with hopes of winning Maria back.

But I only saw her once after my return.

Hello.

Hi.

DINER

She was living with some biker who'd burned all my stuff, including books, artwork, and even the poems I'd written her.

Or so she told me.

He destroyed everything.

Sounds like a nice guy.

I returned home again, realizing once and for all that our relationship was over. I never saw Maria again.

114

Back in Arizona, the tool and die job finally came through.

We do mostly aerospace work here.

Cool.

I bought a little rice rocket motorcycle to get me back and forth to work...

Yamaha RZ 400

...and rented an apartment up on 68th Street and Thomas, my third in less than a year.

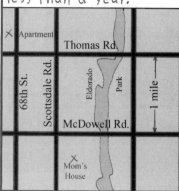

X Apartment

Thomas Rd.

68th St.

Scottsdale Rd.

Eldorado

Park

1 mile

McDowell Rd.

X Mom's House

I also began selling cocaine.

I gotta have a quarter gram on credit. Oh please. I'll do anything.

And of course if I was selling coke, I was also shooting coke.

How many grams did you sell today?

Three. Which means we get one for free. Pass the needles, please.

But oddly enough, I was still free of heroin.

Here you go.

I know. I'm shooting all of my profits...

Which isn't saying much.

...but at least I'm not a junkie.

Cocaine is a chick drug and a poor substitute for heroin. So the fact that it was free wasn't much consolation.

That's great.

Yeah. Wonderful. I'm paranoid, wide awake, horny, and my dick don't work.

115

In truth I was drinking more than anything.

Another one, sir?

But at least you're not a junkie.

Yes, Please. I'm bent on substituting the slobbering inebriation of alcohol for the mellow nihilism of heroin.

Which led me to wreck my motorcycle while riding from a bar to a party late one night.

It was a bad wreck, causing multiple lacerations on my face and head, Plus a broken nose and a lot of road rash.

Is he gonna be all right?

I think so. He's bleeding really bad but he keeps trying to get up and leave.

When I got out of the hospital and saw my face in the mirror, I was convinced my days of getting laid were over.

It was about this time I started using heroin again.

What's this shit?

Mexican black tar heroin.

Not a lot, just a hit here and there on weekends.

Kind of like I did in prison.

My brother Mark, as the youngest sibling, had always been sheltered. By all of us.

I got Mark a Led Zeppelin ticket, too.

Are you crazy? Mom won't let us take him to New York.

Mom often bribed him to keep him out of the trouble the rest of us got into.

If you give up your Zeppelin ticket I'll get you that BB gun.

So when he was growing up, he really didn't have a brother to turn to.

Ask John.

Ask Matt.

I had John, and my sister had aunts Barbara and Beth.

Wanna help me steal us a Christmas tree?

Discount   Menswear
Apparel   Sports
Lingerie   Shoe Sale
Ma   Wanna go   uns
Shopping?

But Mark was often pushed out into the cold.

Who wants to go with your dad to Kentucky?

Not me.

No way.

I'll go.

This was partly under Mom's orders. She wanted him sheltered from all our criminal activity.

I don't want you teaching Mark to steal cars, or sell drugs, or have him hanging out on the streets.

Doing this, though, deprived him of a valuable life lesson.

Can't I go with you guys?

NO!

He never really learned to live on the street.

I'll show all these fuckers.

But Mark, with help from our cousin, Patsy, ended up outdoing all of us.

"You ready?"

"Yep."

He was by far the best shoplifter among us, although none of us knew it at the time.

Insane Sale Tod...

One Day

Or...

"While I distract security, you load up your pockets."

And he began burglarizing houses and stores in our neighborhood at a very young age.

"We're gonna hit Mary's Gift Shop today."

But there are unwritten rules about being a criminal—rules that, because of this protective bubble we'd constructed around him, Mark had never learned.

Rules of Crimininal Procedure

1.) Honor "Honor among thieves."

2.) Never burglarize your neighbor's house.

3.) Never shoplift bologna when roast beef is available.

4.) Don't snitch.

5.) Never shoplift with drugs or other contraband in your pocket.

6.) Don't steal from family and/or friends.

Or he learned them and just didn't give a fuck.

"What about rule 479: 'Don't shit where you sleep'?"

"To hell with the rules."

For years John and his street gang were obsessed with catching the neighborhood burglar.

"We need to catch whoever's doing all these burglaries."

"Yeah, right in our own backyard."

"They're invading our territory."

They never suspected that it was Mark.

MARY'S GIFT SHOP

In 1977, when he was 16, Mark got busted burglarizing a house.

He was wheeling the booty home in a shopping cart when the cops nabbed him.

It was stealing guns that got him in the most trouble. Connecticut had some of the strictest gun laws in the country.

STATE OF
CONNECTICUT
Rules of Criminal
Procedure

Laws Concerning Firearms:

1.) This ain't fucking Texas

And Mark was, at 16, a legal adult and so eligible for prison.

STATE OF
CONNECTICUT
Rules of Criminal
Procedure
Age of consent

1.) The age when a person is considered an adult is 16 years.

Over the next year or so, Mom used a lawyer who owed the family money to try to keep Mark out of prison.

These are serious charges, but I think I can work with the prosecutor.

She and Mark had to fly to Bridgeport from Arizona for his final court date.

This is sentencing for the State of Connecticut v. Mark William Parker.

Mom doesn't remember the deposition. Only that he was spared being sent to prison.

I think we can avoid any jail time in this case...

The State of Connecticut was no doubt happy to be rid of him...

...if you just stay the hell out of Connecticut.

...not to mention the rest of us.

Along with the rest of your larcenous brood.

I don't think Mark ever quite forgave my mother when she moved the family to Arizona from Pennsylvania.

Although glad to be out of Bridgeport, he much preferred the isolated forests of Pennsylvania to the crowded barrenness of greater Phoenix.

But he made the best of it. By the time he was 18 he had a good job and a 1976 Pontiac Firebird.

He loved that car.

I'm a highway star.

At this point in time my family was all but legal.

We'll take it.

FOR SALE

Both my mother and my now stepfather, Carl, had real jobs...

CLASSIFIEDS

Ambassador Suites Hotel	Los Arcos Mall
Now Hiring Inspectors, maids, no experience necessary	Hiring Now Maintenance men, janitors, security personnel
Live-in maids and nannys needed for	Maintenance men wanted

...and that counterfeit money they spent so much time printing was pretty much useless.

How do they look, Marlene?

Like shit.

In early 1984, someone put sugar in the gas tank of Mark's Firebird. His beloved car was ruined.

He then lost his job, which was one of the only jobs he ever had.

I got fired today.

So what?

He couldn't recover from these two events.

But what am I gonna do?

Find another job.

To anyone else in the family these setbacks would have presented nothing more than a minor nuisance.

I hear you lost another job and your car?

Not a big deal. Both are easy to replace.

I even told Mark this.

You get another job, save your money, and buy another car.

I had completely discounted this inability to cope.

I can't.

Bullshit.

I should've put myself in John's shoes.

What's the problem?

How would he have reacted if I'd come to him under similar circumstances?

I'm here for you. No matter what.

When John was murdered in 1980, my mom had him cremated.

What's in that can?

Your brother's ashes.

This bothered Mark, and he told her so.

Why was John cremated?

Well, one reason is that it's cheaper.

I don't ever want to be cremated.

All right.

I was conspicuously absent at John's funeral, hiding inside a syringe in Bridge-port.

Why isn't Matt here?

He couldn't afford to miss work.

But I did send Diane and the baby, hoping that meeting her first grandchild would offer my mother some comfort.

You gonna be Ok here all alone?

I'll be fine.

Not that this was any help to Mark.

What the fuck happened to my brother?

FEBRUAR 1980

We all believe now that Mark didn't cope well with John's death.

I'm Ok.

Everything's cool.

1981

1982

That he suppressed his grief for years.

All's well.

What the fuck happened to my brothers?

1983

1984

122

Mark came to me in the spring of 1984, all but homeless.

I need a place to stay. Carl and mom are all pissed off, and it's hard for me to live there.

I turned him away.

Sorry, but I just can't do it.

I told myself that being tough with Mark was the answer.

Time to grow up. Get out there on your own.

But in truth, I was more concerned with him finding out that I was a junkie.

You turned out your own brother?

What was I supposed to do? I can't let him know I'm a loser.

By this time I had been fired from my tool and die job and was still shooting a lot of cocaine as well as more and more heroin.

Sorry, Mark.

Mark didn't drink or take drugs, although, like my mom, he was a chronic pot smoker.

And because he didn't take real drugs, I didn't want him living in my apartment, which was practically a shooting gallery.

I didn't want him getting that first shot of dope in my house.

Here, Mark. Wanna try some?

Or at least that's what I told myself.

123

Soon after this, Mark returned to Bridgeport, where he learned, through a series of events, exactly what it means to be homeless.

I just need to stay here for a few days, then I'm going up to Maine to live with my dad.

Ok.

Just after he arrived in Connecticut, my aunt Barbara, the lover of Russian literature, died.

He then contacted our father.

I'm here in Bridgeport, and I'd like to come up and stay with you for a while.

Mark always had delusions about our father.

I can go back East and stay with my dad anytime I want. He told me so.

Like a lot of people, he couldn't come to terms with the fact that his parent might be totally indifferent.

Gee, Mark, I'd love to have you, but this is not a good time.

Mark took things like this really hard.

I thought you were going up to Maine to stay with your dad.

So did I.

By September, after three months in Bridgeport, he had hanged himself in a friend's basement.

Hey. Where's Mark?

I haven't seen him all morning.

124

When it came to guilt over Mark, there was plenty to go around.

Everyone, from friends to relatives, feels guilty when a loved one commits suicide.

But who could possibly feel that weight more than the mother?

My mother knows not only what it means to have children but what it means to lose them.

But she kept her word to Mark. He was not cremated, but buried in Scottsdale.

HAROLD JOHN PARKER	MARK WILLIAM PARKER
October 9, 1957 February 1, 1980	July 13, 1961 September 30, 1984
Beloved Sons and Brothers	

When John died, my mother went to a doctor to try to get tranquilizers.

To his credit, he refused her.

Advice I chose to ignore for another 16 years.

Chapter 7

In the summer of 2005, the dean who fired me is herself fired and, without fanfare, I'm given my job back at MCTV.

Why did she fire me in the first place? They told me if I did my probation I'd get my job back.

Who knows? Maybe she just had a thing against ex cons and dirty emails.

MCTV

I'm also working a lot of freelance construction jobs—home repair and remodels and the like.

Hurting financially, Billy becomes my helper...

Let's go, Scrappy.

...and is enchanted by my repertoire of swear words.

Mother-fucking cock-sucking son of a fucking whore.

In exchange for my throwing him this little bone, he sometimes uses me as a roadie.

Let's go, Scrappy.

Ed from Kneedeep and I continue going to concerts...

Who we got this month?

Eric Clapton.

...and I'm getting better at playing the guitar.

Katrina hits New Orleans that same summer, and I get a lesson in otherness lifted right from my ASU textbooks.

A slew of Katrina homeless are shipped to the Veterans Memorial Coliseum in downtown Phoenix.

Walt and Billy arrange a hasty free concert for the refugees and take me along as their roadie.

Let's go, Scrappy.

We meet Governor Janet Napolitano, who was making the rounds.

EXIT

Nice to meet you, Mrs. Mayor.

She's the governor, stupid.

The Coliseum is set up like a prison, complete with armed guards and picture IDs for the refugees.

IDs, Please.

NO AUTHORIZED ENTRY

But the music is sweet, and many are glad for this bit of unfettered attention.

In the fall semester of 2005, I have a girlfriend in Mexico.

Her name is Guadalupe and she lives in Guadalajara.

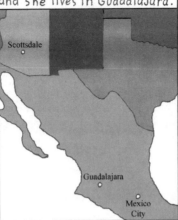

Scottsdale

Guadalajara

Mexico City

My international emails have moved down Mexico way because I don't need a passport to travel there.

Just a birth certificate.

STATE OF
CONNECTICUT
CITY OF
BRIDGEPORT
Certificate of Birth
for
Matthew Joseph Parker
Born the fifth day of April,
1960, to Harold Oliver
Parker and Marlene Gloria
Parker

Saint Vincent's Hospital, Bridgeport, CT

Plus I'm learning Spanish at school, and, let's face it, I live in Arizona.

BIENVENIDOS, GRINGOS, A NOGALES

MOFLES
MUEBLES
ANTIGUOS

HABLAMOS ESPANOL

Guadalupe, or Lupita, is an OB/GYN.

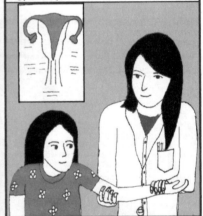

And very sophisticated, preferring the symphony over rock concerts...

...and the theater over movies.

Ser o no ser, ésa es la cuestión.

I like her very much.

After a time I come to love Guadalajara, and Lupita along with it.

Te quiero.

Hmmmf.

Both are cosmopolitan and exotic.

But don't you love me?

No.

You can find restaurants from every country in the city.

SANTO COYOTE

LA FRANCA

DER KRUG BRAUHAUS

Da Napoli

And Lupita travels all over the world to medical conventions.

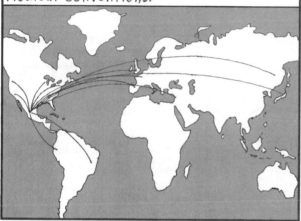

I visit Lupita in Guadalajara every couple of months.

I'm off to Mexico again.

Can't you get laid in Tempe?

And on occasion she visits me here. In the spring of 2006, we drive up to Flagstaff.

What's in Flagstaff?

Trees.

We're supposed to take in the sights but never get out of the hotel room.

You are not finished yet, are you?

I thought I was.

I cum nine times in less than 24 hours.

No no no. Otra vez, por favor.

129

Despite her sexual appetite, Lupita could be distant and aloof.

Sex is the most vibrant form of love.

What?

And although I'm getting a fair measure of intimacy from her, love is conspicuously absent.

Do you want to make love?

No. Sexo solo.

Lupita is too busy for love.

No. You cannot visit. I'm going to Tel Aviv.

Not that this is an altogether bad thing.

Well, I sure love to fuck...

But it's difficult for me to be little more than a pleasant interlude in her life.

...but I feel objectified.

¿Cómo?

I'm starting to realize that I'm not someone she would ever take home to her parents, although it was probably clear from the beginning.

My prison tattoos embarrass her, and she bitches about my cigarette smoking.

No puedes fumar en mi coche.

In response, I cling harder, which only pushes her away further.

My main problem is that, in my 46 years, I've never had a normal relationship.

You are the first normal woman I've ever dated.

No soy normal, gringo puto.

In the summer of 2006, Lupita visits me in Arizona.

I take her to a club where Billy is playing, outdoors on the patio.

Most of my friends are there.

I present Billy with an early birthday present—a portrait in pen and ink.

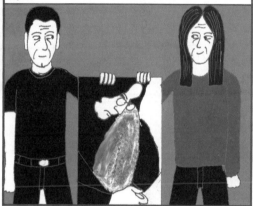

Lupita loves my friends and family.

I'm having a really good time, but...

But she's incapable of loving me. Lupita is basically a sex partner.

...fuck me and send me home.

131

After Mark's death in September of 1984, I took to heroin with a vengeance.

Time-released suicide in a syringe.

After getting canned from my tool and die job, I was back working construction.

You're fired! We need sober tool makers, not some rehabbed construction worker.

I also folded my minor cocaine business.

How come you stopped selling coke?

Too much heat. I'm scared of prison.

I lost another apartment because I spent the rent money on dope.

EVICTION

NOTICE

All junkies and and other sundry lowlifes must vacate the premises immediately.

The Sheriff of Sottingham

I was a junkie. Again.

We need dope money, baby. Why don't you rob somebody?

Fucking amateur.

Eventually I moved in with a girlfriend named Sarah...

It's all right, baby. I'll buy tonight—if you come live with me.

JNk 139

...whom I was incapable of loving.

I love you, baby.

Ummmf.

She was basically a dope-shooting partner...

You know I can't fix myself, baby. You have to do it for me.

As long as you're buying.

...who happened to be good in bed.

Now you just lie back and relax and let me do all the work.

132

We let another junkie, Heather, move in with us.

Can I stay with you guys for a while?

I don't know...

Sure you can.

She was a full-time titty dancer and part-time prostitute.

Five bucks for a lap dance, 150 for a fuck.

Threesomes became a nightly ritual.

Heroin makes us horny.

This was not my first indulgence in ménage à trois, but it would be my last.

Eat my pussy.

No. You eat mine.

Lick my nuts.

No. You first.

I don't want to lick your nuts, I want my pussy licked by her.

Fuck your pussy.

Hello. I'm being ignored.

First off, it's an utterly overrated sexual act.

I'm sorry for ignoring you.

Here, have a tit.

Let's see yous shoot up without me.

That's all right.

Mmmm. that's good.

A guy's only got one dick, after all.

We're sorry.

Yeah. Come over here and fuck me.

No. Fuck me.

But my pussy is better.

He's not fucking you first. He's my boyfriend.

And secondly, dealing with one junkie girlfriend was bad enough, but two?

We wanna get high. Can't you go rob somebody?

133

I also stayed at Mom's house on occasion.

I need to get away from those crazy women for a while.

Take Mark's room.

It was in this room that I found a duffel bag full of counterfeit 100-dollar bills.

Where's the best place to stash all this funny money?

In the room where the junkie sleeps.

Mom's last gasp at criminality.

These bills don't look real.

No shit. Guess we'll have to get real jobs.

I took about 20 grand back to our apartment but was wary about passing them.

Wow. Look at all that money. Let's go spend some.

Stupid. You can't just pass these anywhere.

All the bills had the same serial number.

Sarah and Heather, however, had no such inhibitions.

Wow! Look at all that money. Where can we pass some?

Anywhere we want.

They took some bills without my knowledge and began passing them around the neighborhood.

This is just a block from the apartment.

So what?

All right. Let's go.

Bringing the heat down on all of us.

We have two women on film passing these hundreds at a Smitty's.

Yeah, but they ain't the source. Let's check out the boyfriend.

DEPARTMENT of the TREASURY

I noticed I was being followed by men in suits, who turned out to be Secret Service agents.

So I confronted Sarah, and she confessed.

What the fuck did you do?

We took some of that money and spent it.

They had been passing the bills mostly in the Phoenix suburb of Mesa, on one occasion mere yards from our apartment.

Why didn't you just pay the fucking rent with it?

I waited for the feds to kick down our door, but they never did.

Get everything out of the apartment. Hurry.

Scared and confused, I went to my mom, and together we decided to get rid of all the counterfeit money.

Let's just bag it up and throw it in a dumpster.

No. Our fingerprints are all over it.

I wish we could just burn it.

Wait. We can. Come with me.

$300,000 torched in the backyard barbecue.

Phew. It reeks.

That's all right. But what happened to the gas?

The grill never worked again.

I think the ink is clogging the jets.

Hmmm. Pass me that lighter fluid.

135

Sarah and I soon lost the apartment, and I moved back in with Mom.

EVICTION NOTICE

All junkies and other lowlifes are encouraged to run back home to their mommies.

The Sheriff of mommingham

Going through some old clothes, I found five of the counterfeit hundreds in the pocket of some pants.

Hey. What's this?

I should have destroyed them right then, but didn't.

I need to get rid of these.

But wait. Maybe I can do something with them.

I was a junkie, after all, and the bills represented a potential fix.

But I had all those feds on me. Is it worth it?

Oh. You're just being paranoid. You'll just have to be extra careful.

Some months later, I got a call from Heather.

Hey. How've you been?

OK I guess.

She wanted to trade heroin, straight across, for counterfeit bills.

Listen. I'll give you heroin in exchange for some of those fake 100-dollar bills.

I don't know. You already put me through enough crap with those bills. Besides, I got rid of them all.

I put her off at first because I didn't trust her. But she kept calling back.

Hi. It's me again. I still need some of those bills.

Sorry. They're all gone.

She got me on the day after Thanksgiving, 1985.

Matt? You have a phone call.

Things were going relatively well, and on that day, I was as high as Everest.

What seek you, my child?

Counterfeit money.

← 29,029 feet

I wasn't thinking too clear, what with all that thin air UP there.

Why certainly, my child. I happen to have five crisp bills to trade for a bit of Nirvana.

I agreed to meet her at Suds City, a bar in Tempe.

SUDS CITY

When I pulled into the parking lot, I noticed a van—the kind sometimes used for surveillance.

Every nerve in my body screamed for me to drive away.

Run away.

Fly, you fool.

It's a setup.

Get out while the getting's good.

But I convinced myself that I was just being paranoid.

Oh, fuck it. What could happen?

I parked and walked into the bar.

Mom remortgaged the house in 2004 and, with her help, I bought a Harley that December.

Here's 11 grand. You can pay me back in increments.

Thanks, Mom.

A 1987 FXST Wide Glide with mini ape-hanger handlebars.

I take Lupita for a ride on it, but she isn't impressed.

Not that it matters. We break up soon after Billy's birthday bash in the summer of 2006.

Even though we are no longer lovers, I think we can remain friends.

I got enough friends, thanks just the same.

When school begins a month later, I decide to ride the bike from work at SCC to school at ASU.

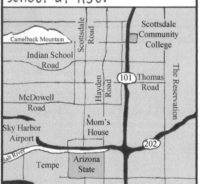

Camelback Mountain
Scottsdale Road
Scottsdale Community College
Indian School Road
Hayden Road
101 Thomas Road
The Reservation
McDowell Road
Sky Harbor Airport
Mom's House
Salt River
Tempe
Arizona State
202

Because the price of gas is through the roof, and my pickup truck is a guzzler.

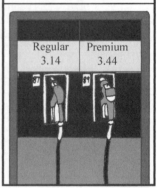

| Regular 3.14 | Premium 3.44 |

But Harleys are cruisers.

They aren't designed for putting around through city traffic, particularly the Phoenix metro area.

PAYDAY LOANS

People drive like idiots here.

PRAY FOR ME
I DRIVE ON
SCOTTSDALE ROAD

On September 19, I'm riding south on Hayden Road, heading to ASU after work.

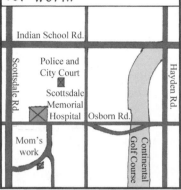

I'm doing about 50, just 5 mph over the speed limit. It's early, about 11:30 a.m., and traffic is light.

An 86-year-old woman pulls out from a strip mall, right in front of me, just south of Osborn Road.

I try going around her to my left, but it's obvious she doesn't see me because she keeps coming, driving me into oncoming traffic.

The only thing I can do is lock the brakes and lay the bike down on its side.

When I hit her, I'm catapulted upward, smashing the right side of my body and head into the driver's side of her car.

I fall to the ground, unconscious.

I wake up to paramedics hovering over me.

You're going to be fine. Can you tell me where it hurts?

MY whole right side is hurting.

Where does it hurt?

My hip.

Ok, don't move. What's your name?

I can't remember who I am, and I get tired of them asking me. So I hand them my wallet.

What's your name?

I don't remember. Here, look for yourself.

Don't move.

I can't think through the pain in my side. My head is pounding, and everything appears foggy. The questioning continues.

What day is it?

What year is it?

Who's the president?

I don't know.

I don't know.

Fucking Bush.

Once they're satisfied that I'm reasonably coherent, they take me to Scottsdale Memorial Hospital.

While still in the emergency room, I get a visit from the cop investigating the accident.

I gave the other driver a ticket for failure to yield.

Then State welfare because I don't have health insurance.

We need to get you on AHCCCS.

Whatever.

Followed by my mom, who hovers anxiously, as if to convince herself that I'm not seriously injured.

Ready for some morphine?

My injuries are the opposite of the ones I suffered in the accident I had back in 1984.

My whole body aches.

Relax. They're gonna do some tests on you.

And this one happened mere blocks from the other one.

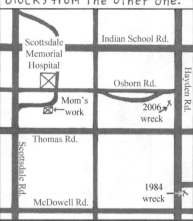

Scottsdale Memorial Hospital

Indian School Rd.

Osborn Rd.

Hayden Rd.

Mom's work

2006 wreck

Scottsdale Rd.

Thomas Rd.

1984 wreck

McDowell Rd.

Then all my injuries were superficial—deep gashes and cuts on my face.

I'll never get laid again.

This time they're all internal—a fractured hip, bruised kidney and back, along with a lacerated liver and a major concussion.

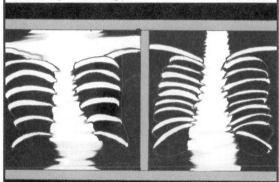

Once I get a room they tell me I'll likely be released in the morning. I'm not sure if this is because I have no health insurance.

We'll keep you overnight for observation and send you home tomorrow.

Mom is there for most of my stay, seemingly more scared of the morphine than she is of my injuries.

I'm not gonna relapse, Mom.

That's because I'm in pretty good shape, considering.

How you feeling?

I hurt all over, but my head is clear.

We both know that if I'd hit that car head-on, I likely would've been killed.

Thank God you know how to ride.

Advantages of an unconventional upbringing.

Soon after the accident, I surf the Web for Latinas, skipping over Mexico this time and concentrating on Colombia.

Almost immediately I begin emailing Nataly, a woman from the southern city of Cali.

Being poor and Colombian, however, a U.S. visa is out of the question for her.

American Consulate in Bogotá
Carrera 45
Bogotá, Colombia

Dear Colombiana,
We regret to inform you that we do not provide tourist visas to poor Latinas. Try again when you get a bank account and maybe some property.

Sincerely,
The Gringos

So in January I cut a deal with the State of Connecticut.

STATE OF CONNECTICUT
Department of Social Services
Child Support Division

Dear Matthew Parker,

I'm afraid we cannot allow you to obtain a U.S. passport until you have satisfied all of your debt obligations to the Child Support Division of the

I agree to pay them half of what I owe.

STATE OF CONNECTICUT
Department of Social Services
Child Support Division

Plea bargain reached in which Matthew Parker agrees to pay half of his back child support owed, approximately $4,200, in exchange for total alleviation of any and all past debts.

This satisfies my obligation, and I am able to get a passport.

STATE OF CONNECTICUT
Department of Social Services
Child Support Division

Dear Matthew Parker,

You are now cleared to obtain your passport. See how much easier things can be when you are able to pay your debts?

Back in 2003, I obtained a bank account and even a couple of credit cards.

Now I even have a passport and have become an ex con cliché.

Much to my chagrin.

Nataly is beautiful but wary of men.

No tengo confianza en hombres.

¿Por qué?

She's been hurt too much in the past by all that Latino machismo.

Son mentirosos.

No todos.

On my first trip in March of 2007, she is unsure of how she feels about me, especially my tattoos.

Es del Diablo, ¿No?

No.

But I try to be romantic and pleasant and begin to grow on her...

Mmmmmmm. Me gusta tus besos.

Lo sé.

...although she makes it clear from the start that sex is out of the question.

But no sex, for now. When you return in July I will be ready.

Shit.

Still, she is lovably huggable and we smooch like teenagers, which, in a pleasant irony, is exactly what I've been craving.

"Pussy-whipped" is an alien concept to me.

Dude, I am totally pussy-whipped.

I have no clue what that's like.

But I often thought it would be nice.

One pussy's whipping boy is just another pussy's guy.

143

It was the day after Thanksgiving in 1985 when I took Heather out behind the Suds City bar and traded her counterfeit hundreds for heroin.

A quarter gram for five of those bills, right?

Right.

I then went and played a game of pinball while finishing my beer.

EXIT

SPUD   BOOZE

I had a wedding to go to, although I can't remember whose wedding.

One quick game and I'm outta here.

SPUD

Or why they would invite a junkie.

GUEST
LIST
for the wedding of

_____

&

_____

Bride's Family:

Groom's Family:

Junkies:

Not that it mattered. I was arrested a few minutes later.

Drop the flippers and step away from the machine.

TILT

It turned out that the only people in that bar who were not Secret Service agents were the bartender and Heather.

I'll never know for sure, but I had my suspicions that Heather was working with the feds.

SUPER SECRET SERVICE

They threw me in the back of an unmarked car and we headed east.

I was so high that they had to stop the car and let me puke.

Hold him.

Fuck. He splattered my shoes.

When we arrived at the Mesa Police station, they gave me sodas and cigarettes and a trash can to puke in...

Relax. Have a smoke.

We know that you smoke.

...and proceeded to pepper me with questions.

Where'd you get the bills?

Where are the plates?

As a junkie, I was not only the best liar in the world but also the fastest.

Do you know any Hell's Angels in Florida?

How about Vegas?

I couldn't tell the truth without ratting on my family, so I made up a story on the spot.

I found the bills in that old abandoned lighthouse down at Seaside Park in Bridgeport.

And then what?

They let both me and Heather go later that night, with a promise that I'd show up at the Federal Building in downtown Phoenix the following Monday.

We'll release you now if you promise to take a lie detector test on Monday.

We need to make sure you are telling us the truth.

I don't know if she set me up, but I had told her to come alone, and she didn't.

Did you not hear me when I said come alone, you stupid cunt?

I didn't know he was a cop. Wanna come crash at my place?

145

It was Mom who took me down to the Federal Building the following Monday.

Want a hit?

No.

19972

She also straightened me out.

Don't take a lie detector test. Tell them to arrest you or fuck off.

This is exactly what I did.

I'm not taking your stupid test, and I want a fucking lawyer.

They let me go and in-indicted me 10 months later.

UNITED STATES DISTRICT COURT
DISTRICT OF ARIZONA

United States of America,
          Plaintiff,

vs.

Matthew Parker,
          Defendant.

CASE NO. AZUSM0100
Grand Jury Indictment

Dealing in Counterfeit Obligations
Conspiracy to Deal in Counterfeit Obligations
Possession of Heroin

On November 29, 1985, the defendant, Matthew Parker, exchanged five (5) counterfeit one-hundred (100) dollar bills for approximately 1 quarter gram of heroin at the Suds City Bar, located at 198 McClintock Road in Tempe, Arizona. Mr. Parker was under surveillance by agents from the U.S. Department of the Treasury and, after making the exchange, was arrested and taken to the

I turned myself in and was released under conditions on my own recognizance.

I'm going to release you, Mr. Parker, but you'll have to submit to random drug testing.

But my supplying them with drug-free pee turned out to be problematic.

URINANALYSIS TESTING LAB
San Francisco, California

Urinanalysis test results for: Matthew Parker

Positive for morphine, which indicates heroin or other opiate ingestion by the subject, or perhaps he ate a shitload of poppy seeds.

The judge then ordered me into a pretrial rehab—Behavioral Systems Southwest.

You need to kick your drug habit, Mr. Parker, and this halfway house is designed to help.

I was allowed to go to work and report back to the rehab each night, which made it easy to maintain my habit.

Welcome home, Mr. Parker. Time for your nightly piss.

MEN

In January of 1987, the U.S. Marshals came in and arrested me for failing my mandatory drug test.

You're under arrest for dirty urine.

What? I'm supposed to stop being a junkie overnight simply because a judge ordered it?

Chapter 8

I apply to Columbia for grad school, as well as Rutgers and ASU, in the fall of 2006. All three grad school applications are for MFAs in creative writing.

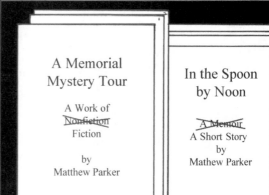

RUTGERS
Application for the 2007-2008 Academic Year

Master of F~~~
Creative W~~~
Nonfiction~~~
to do list
3 letters of
writing sampl~

Arizona State University

Graduate Degree Programs

~applications for graduate
~cember 10,
~te School
~n poetry and
~have a MFA
~for writers of
~e get bent

Columbia University School of the Arts
Application for Master of Fine Arts (MFA) degree in creative writing

I have to submit my nonfiction as fiction at ASU because they don't have an MFA nonfiction program.

A Memorial Mystery Tour

A Work of ~~Nonfiction~~ Fiction

by
Matthew Parker

In the Spoon by Noon

~~A Memoir~~
A Short Story
by
Mathew Parker

Applying to grad school is like having an extra class with, of course, the obligatory extra fees.

Class Schedule
Fall 2007, ASU

African Ame
History
Thesis Prepa
Creative non
Grad School
Applications

Application Fees:
ASU $50
Columbia $50
Rutgers $50

I have to write a thesis to graduate from Barrett, the Honors College, and have chosen to focus on Literary Darwinism.

The Altruism Equation
Seven Scientists Search for the Origin of Goodness
Lee Alan Dugatkin

On the Origin of Species
Charles Da~~~

The Selfish Gene
Richard Dawkins

Madame Bovary's Ovaries
A Darwinian Look at Literature
David P. & Nanelle R. Barash

Unto Others
The Evolution and Psychology of Unselfish Behavior
Elliot Sober and David Sloan Wilson

The Evolution of Darwinism
Selection, Adaptation and Progress in Evolutionary Biology
Timothy Shanahan

This only makes my task harder, in that I now have to defend my thesis before two departments.

Department of English

School of Life Science

Who don't always see eye to eye.

Nurture!

Nature!

A few years back at SCC, I was thinking of changing my major to science.

Anyone who's been to prison would be naturally interested in a relatively faster way through time.

Einstein-Rosen ___e

$ds^2 = -c^2dt^2 + dl^2 + (k^2$ ___ $) + sin^2\theta d($

traver___ble

Specifically, astro-physics.

The randomness inherent in quantum physics is even more postmodern than heroin.

Albert Einstein is one of my main heroes.

Only two things are infinite, the universe and human stupidity... and I'm not sure about the universe.

Along with Niels Bohr...

Your theory is crazy, but not crazy enough to be true.

...Chuck Yeager...

Most pilots learn... that one thing you don't do, you don't believe anything anybody tells you about an airplane.

...Alan Shepard...

It's a very sobering feeling to be up in space and realize that one's safety factor was determined by the lowest bidder on a government contract.

...and Carl Sagan.

A celibate clergy is an especially good idea, because it tends to suppress any hereditary propensity toward fanaticism.

Back at SCC, I once said to my astronomy professor, Steve Mutz, that I believed all earthly mysteries had been solved.

Don't ever let a biology professor hear you say that.

Kepler's L___

Newt___

$F = ma$

He was, of course, correct.

The Prisoner's Dilemma

by

Albert W. Tucker

A Paradox in Game Theory

148

I took a basic physics class with Professor Mutz, just to see how I'd do, but I had to drop it.

Mr. Parker, can you give us a simple mathematical explanation of Newton's third law?

Not in a million light-years.

I understood the movement of matter through space-time on a physical level...

Newton's Third Law: For every action there is an equal and opposite... ...reaction!

...but not on a theoretical level.

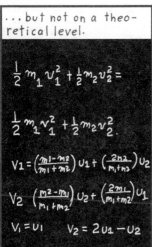

$$\frac{1}{2}m_1 v_1^2 + \frac{1}{2}m_2 v_2^2 =$$

$$\frac{1}{2}m_1 v_1^2 + \frac{1}{2}m_2 v_2^2.$$

$$V_1 = \left(\frac{m_1 - m_2}{m_1 + m_2}\right)U_1 + \left(\frac{2m_2}{m_1 + m_2}\right)U_2$$

$$V_2 \left(\frac{m_2 - m_1}{m_1 + m_2}\right)U_2 + \left(\frac{2m_1}{m_1 + m_2}\right)U_1$$

$$V_1 = U_1 \qquad V_2 = 2U_1 - U_2$$

My math, as has been noted, sucks.

Mr. Parker, can you simplify this equation?

Sure. If you've got about a week.

So I decided to major in English Literature.

MILTON

NORTON ANTHOLOGY of English Literature The Middle Ages

PARADISE LOST

SHAKESPEARE

I could build you a spaceship but never design one.

ACME SPACESHIP DESIGN inc

specs

As much as I love the mysteries inherent in space and quantum physics, writing is where my talent lay.

RECENT PUBLICATION HISTORY

Nonfiction in "LUX," May 2006
Poem in ASU's undergraduate anthology, "Marooned," April 2005
Short story in ASU's undergraduate anthology, "Marooned," November 2004
Short story in Scottsdale Community College's annual anthology, "Vortex," May 2004
Poem and short story in Scottsdale Community College's annual anthology, "Vortex," May 2003
Editorial in the "Scottsdale Tribune," September, 2002

When I transferred to ASU, I got interested in life science because of the words of Professor Mutz.

There are plenty of terrestial mysteries left to be solved.

You could spend decades studying the human mind alone.

Kepler's Laws

Newton

F=ma

And because Darwin was also one of my heroes.

If the misery of the poor be caused not by the laws of nature, but by our institutions, great is our sin.

So I took an honors class on evolutionary biology.

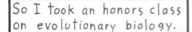

Evidentialism dictates that belief in God must be supported by objective evidence.

Darwin creation Malthus

Darwin's Bulldog

Huxley

My professor was John Lynch.

Any belief is rational only if there is evidence to support it, and rationality is in direct proportion to the balance of the evidence.

Darwinism creationis Malthus

Darwin's Bulldog Huxley

Prince kropotki

And he got me interested in literary Darwinism.

We rarely look to biology to explain human behavior.

I like it because it holds literary theory to task.

Darwinism offers an alternative to literary theory that has its foundation in nature...

Particularly John Locke's tabula rasa.

...rather than nurture.

You just can't so easily get around Darwin.

Things like sexual selection are observable, while Locke's blank slates are not.

By the time I checked into Behavioral Systems Southwest in the winter of 1987, more than a year after I was originally busted, I already had one foot in the cell door.

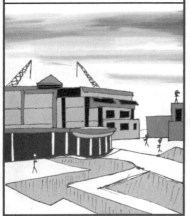

I can't pee with you standing there watching me.

That's fine. We'll just put it down as a dirty.

I was working for Joe Mellencamp at the time as an apprentice electrician.

Did you know he's John Mellencamp's brother?

No. But now that you mention it, they do look a lot alike.

The job was a new Hyatt in north Scottsdale.

In late January I got back to the halfway house at the usual time.

To All Residents
Check-in Rules

I fixed a nice speedball, then stashed another one, loaded in a syringe, in the closet of my room.

I had just finished eating when the U.S. Marshals came in and arrested me.

They took me right to the Towers Jail...

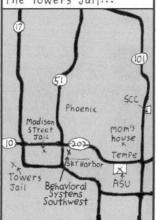

... where, the following day, I got 10 days in the hole for writing my name on a holding-cell door.

Matt Parker

It would be my one experience with solitary confinement out of all the time I'd do. I guess it was good to get it out of the way early on.

Maricopa County Sheriff's Office
Inmate Disciplinary Report
Towers Jail

<u>C01-Destruction of State Property</u>

(Guilty) Not Guilty

Sanction 10 days disciplinary segregation

And it was for such a bullshit reason.

There's hundreds of names written in that cell.

Yes. But you were stupid enough to write your full name.

I had my own cell but was climbing the walls because I had no cigarettes.

The county provided free tobacco back in those days, but not to guys who were doing hole time.

Maricopa County Sheriff's Office
Inmate Indigent Supply Form
Towers Jail

✓ Shower shoes
✓ Toothbrush and toothpaste
✓ Soap
✓ Razor
✓ Comb
✓ Writing paper
✓ Five (5) pre-stamped envelopes
✗ Tobacco (Note: only provided to those inmates not under disciplinary sanctions)

I was also on LOP, which meant I couldn't buy any.

Maricopa County Sheriff's Office
Loss of Privileges Canteen List*

✓ Soap
✓ Shampoo
✓ Conditioner
✓ Stamps
✓ Writing tablet
✓ Deodorant

*Only 10 dollars per week can be spent on the above items. No food or tobacco products can be purchased on LOP, although the more creative among you can make LOP hors d'oeuvres; e.g., toothpaste spread over stamps. Yum yum.

I tried bumming one off a guard who smoked constantly on her walks.

Can I bum a cigarette from you?

I can't give out cigarettes to inmates.

She wouldn't give me one, but a few walks later she tossed a box of tobacco into my cell.

It was pure nectar.

I only had one book—some awful World War II romance novel that I read four times.

NIGHT SKY

Clare Francis

After I did my 10 days, I was put in population.

Anybody got any good books?

Here's one called "Still Life with Woodpecker."

I learned that jail was just a holding facility for inmates making their way through the court system.

This is the lowest rung of the incarceration ladder.

I was being held with no bond because I violated the terms of my release.

And if you never wanna come back here you'll go to prison and do your time and just get it over with.

After two months locked up, I was sentenced to three years probation and released.

You took the probation?

Yep.

Yer a fool. You'll be back here before you know it.

Not if I can help it.

That's the whole point. You can't. Yer a junkie.

They let me out at midnight and, after getting drunk at a bar first, I snuck back into my old room at the halfway house and retrieved the speedball I had stashed there.

I tried to do probation, but the rules were too hard for me.

Terms of Probation
You must work on the books.
Report five mornings weekly to TERROS to take the opium blocker Trexane.
Report to TERROS three times a week for urinalysis.
Report to TERROS four nights a week for drug rehab meetings.
No driving allowed due to revoked driver's license, even though we realize TERROS is 18 miles from your house and public transportaion is dismal.

It didn't take me long to get strung out.

You're due at TERROS in an hour.

Fuck TERROS. I need heroin.

Ditching probation, I went on the run, trying to dodge a federal fugitive of justice warrant.

And fuck probation, too. They'll catch me when they can.

153

I fled back to Bridge-port in December of 1987. There was no airport security in those days. You could fly without an ID even.

Sky Harbor International Airport

Security Checkpoint

It was cold and I was home-less and I found that I had very few friends.

I need a place to crash tonight.

Sorry, man. Can't help you.

When I was out of money and out of dope, I called Sarah.

I need to come home, baby. It's freezing here and I miss you and I need a fucking fix.

She flew me back to Phoenix and met me at the airport with a loaded syringe. I lasted in Bridgeport barely two weeks.

Ahhhh. That Arizona sun sure feels good.

This will warm you up even more.

I then hid out at a friend's house up in Paradise Valley...

You're hiding out at Kim's, you fucker.

Relax. The marshals are hunting for me.

Yeah, but you don't need to hide out with that cunt.

Oh no? Where else should I hide? At your parents'?

...where the marshals even-tually tracked me down a month or so later.

You're under arrest for probation violation.

No shit.

It was Sarah who told them where I was.

Sure. I know where he is. Would you like me to draw you a map?

They locked me back up in the Towers on a pro-bation hold.

Welcome back, Parker. You lasted less than a year.

Yeah, well, heroin and probation don't mix.

154

It was exactly the same—overcrowded and violent—except for the faces.

County jails were designed with discomfort in mind. The food was barely edible and the portions small.

What is it?

Better not to know.

We were always hungry in the Towers.

Look at that cheeseburger.

I forget how they taste.

Snacks could be purchased from the commissary, but it was all junk food and did little to satisfy hunger.

Maricopa County Sheriff's Office Commisary List		
	Price	Quantity
Candy bars	45	6
Chips	45	6
Honey buns	60	4
Pecan pies	60	2
Cookies	45	6
Crackers (cheese)	45	10
Crackers (peanut butter)	45	
Corn nuts	50	5

By this point I had decided to just go to prison and do my time. I would never make it on probation. I liked heroin too much.

So you won't let them reinstate your probation?

Fuck no. I'll do my two years, then after that I can shoot all the dope I want.

The judge sentenced me to two years in federal prison.

We want the defendant to do the full three years, Your Honor.

But it's his first offense. How about two?

A couple of weeks later, I was transferred to the Federal Correctional Institution just north of Phoenix.

INMATE HANDBOOK

Federal Correctional Institution
Phoenix, AZ

I had made it to the fed joint.

CONTENTS

Waiting to hear from Columbia had been almost unbearable.

It's no fun when your entire future is in the hands of strangers. It's like waiting in the county jail to get sentenced.

Now I can relax and concentrate on my graduation in May and writing my thesis.

This is when a lot of honor students drop out of Barretts. They just can't handle writing a 50-page paper in their last semester.

I decide to do Darwinian themes in Ken Kesey's novel "Sometimes a Great Notion."

And don't just concentrate on modern-day Darwinism. Read "Descent of Man" and other contemporaries of Darwin.

Literary Darwinism is packed with biological determinism, which is anathema to conventional literary theorists.

We abhor the inflexibility inherent in sociobiology and evolutionary psychology.

Literary Theory

But to me it makes sense.

Elementary, my dear deconstructionists. Elementary.

In my thesis, I concentrate on a question that puzzled Charles Darwin, and indeed puzzles Darwinists to this day.

Why are people kind to each other? Why haven't I killed my neighbor and stolen his wife and Porsche?

Darwin's theory of natural selection is fierce, competitive, and, by its character, selfish.

Give me that ox leg and all your women, you fucking ape.

Go take a flying fuck at a rolling wheel, you baboon.

There appears to be no room in natural selection for selfless acts of kindness.

Why can't we all just...   Shut up.

Doink!

Natural selection functions on the level of the individual.

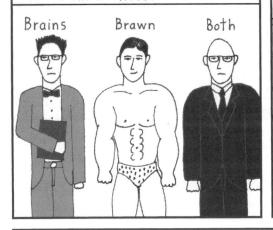

Brains   Brawn   Both

The fastest cheetah, say, is more likely to survive, thus passing on her fast genes to her progeny.

But if selection profits the individual and his/her offspring alone, then why do certain insects like ants and bees produce droves of sterile workers?

We can't sing.

We can't fuck.

But we think we can dance.

Further, why will such individuals willingly sacrifice their life for the good of the hive or colony?

You go on. I'll hold off the bee keeper.

But you can't sting your way out of this.

It's the survival of the hive that counts.

I suppose. Even that whore of a queen.

In "On the Origin of Species," Darwin explains how the sterility of insects can be selected for.

This difficulty, though appearing insuperable, is lessened, or...disappears, when it is remembered that selection may be applied to the individual as well as to the family.

There are three theories that attempt to explain how altruism can be naturally selected: kin selection, group selection, and reciprocal altruism.

I'll save my child's life before that of a stranger, and even look out for the interests of my peer group...

...but why in the fuck should I ever be kind to a person I don't know?

The first, kin selection, was formalized by W.D. Hamilton in 1964.

Building on Darwin's idea of selection operating on the family level...

Help!

...Hamilton postulates that even though an altruist may sacrifice its own reproductive fitness to enhance that of a relative...

Christ. I almost drowned saving your ass. And you just a second cousin.

...it is likely that this relative will carry at least a portion of the altruist's genes.

Yes. But I carry your genes. Just look how small our penises are.

The second theory, group selection, was expounded upon by Sewall Wright.

He theorized that altruism can be selected for in different groups, but only if these groups occasionally mix for breeding purposes.

Do you mind if I cross territorial lines to fuck your sister?

Be my guest.

But the third, reciprocal altruism, is to my mind the most brilliant and was written by a guy named Robert Trivers.

His idea is that acts of kindness between strangers can enjoy reproductive success if such acts are eventually reciprocated.

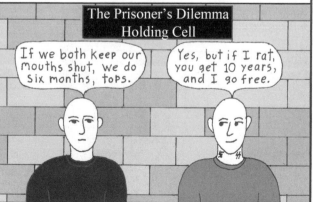

The Prisoner's Dilemma Holding Cell

If we both keep our mouths shut, we do six months, tops.

Yes, but if I rat, you get 10 years, and I go free.

Being moved from the county jail to the Federal Correctional Institution, (FCI) Phoenix, was a bit of a shock.

There were tiled floors, carpeting, and soft, cushy chairs in the dayroom, and even seats on the toilets.

The food was good, or at least edible, and there was plenty of it.

Please, sir, have some more.

Don't mind if I do.

FCI Phoenix was a medium security prison.

I was in a reception area called Yuma Unit, where I was classified as minimum security and designated to be shipped out to the Federal Prison Camp (FPC) in Boron, California.

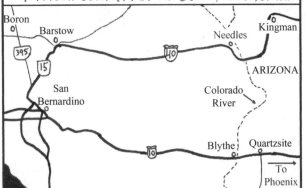

In Yuma Unit, we were locked down most of the time as hundreds of inmates were shuffled through this prison way station.

After a couple weeks I was able to buy two hits of LSD for a carton of cigarettes.

Don't tell your cellie. With all this coming and going, you never know who's a snitch around here.

I dropped them in my cell one morning and tripped my balls off for hours.

Ha ha ha ha ha ha ha ha ha.

I'm locked up with a crazy man.

160

After a few weeks they rolled me and about ten other guys up to be moved.

They're moving us tomorrow.

How do you know?

Phones are shut off. They don't want us planning an escape on the road.

And drove us in vans to FCI Terminal Island, or TI for short.

Terminal Island

To Los Angeles

Pacific Ocean

To Long Beach

We were housed in a lockdown unit called J-1, which was basically a built-in county jail.

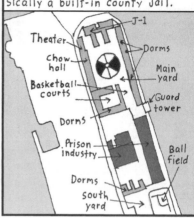

J-1

Theater

Chow hall

Basketball courts

Dorms

Prison industry

Dorms

South yard

Dorms

Main yard

Guard tower

Ball field

This was a real prison, much older, and more stereotypically prisonlike than FCI Phoenix. It was at TI, as I stared up at three tiers of cells, that it finally hit me. I was in prison and wasn't getting out for some time.

But when I sneaked out on the yard, I found out that sentenced inmates like me were not supposed to be housed in J-1.

J-1 is just a holding cell for courts.

File on them.

So what can I do about it?

So the next day I filed a grievance and they moved me out on the yard quick.

Roll your shit up, Parker, you're moving out of here.

Cool.

I went from being locked down and double-bunked in crowded, noisy, violent J-1 to a single bed in a quiet dorm.

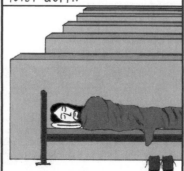

A dorm I could come and go from any time the yard was open.

Where you heading?

I don't know. Maybe the library.

The drawback was that when the guards from Boron came to pick us up, I was left behind.

Where's Parker; 19972-008?

He's out on the yard.

Well, we ain't waiting.

And the money I had on my books at FCI Phoenix was lost in limbo somewhere.

Any idea where my money is?

Probably Talladega.

Counselor Office Hours
M-F 8:00 - 11:30
12:30 - 3:30

I was stuck there for a month, but it wasn't an issue, as I could hustle what I needed to survive.

How much you want to draw a birthday card for my wife?

Two pouches of tobacco an a bar of soap.

TI was live with stabbings, burglaries, and drugs.

Why is the yard locked down again?

Another stabbing and the commissary was burglarized.

I should've known.

Want a hit?

But I didn't care. I loved the ocean smell and the goofy gulls perched unconcerned on the massive razor-wire fences...

...or circling the guard towers.

A few weeks later the guards from Boron showed up to take me to my new home.

Let's go, Parker.

It's about time.

Then you should've stayed in J-1.

We drove right through Glen Helen Park, the site of the 1983 US Festival.

Glen Helen Pk.
↓
EXIT ONLY

Boron was located about 70 miles north of Ontario and 40 miles west of Barstow.

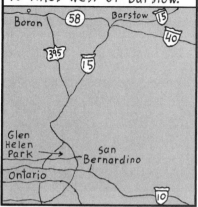

It was high-desert country where the wind blew constantly.

But as prisons go, it wasn't much of one.

Both the FCIs of Phoenix and TI had double fences brimming with razor wire.

FPC Boron, by comparison, didn't even have a fence, just a yellow line painted around it.

Look! I'm escaping.

OUT OF BOUNDS

There was no real violence at Boron because everyone was short to the gate—within a few years of going home. We were all wino-timers.

How much time you got left?

37 days and a wake-up.

And the food was excellent, with a baked potato bar or pasta bar available on week-days, as a side to the main lunch menu.

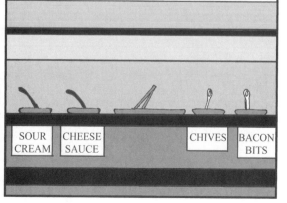

SOUR CREAM

CHEESE SAUCE

CHIVES

BACON BITS

In the spring semester of 2007 I successfully defend my thesis before biology professor John Lynch and English Professors Elizabeth McNeil and Heather Hoyt.

Congratulations. Excellent defense.

Elizabeth is also my ASU adviser, and a good friend. She often accompanies me to see kneedeep, Billy, and/or Walt perform.

I remodeled both of her bathrooms over the last few years.

No, Billy. Lift it by the bowl, not the tank.

In May I have two separate graduation ceremonies: the smaller one, from the Honors College, is held at Grady Gammage Auditorium, and my more general graduation is held in the much larger Wells Fargo Arena.

In the audience at Gammage are my mom and sister, Billy and Gwen, along with Amy Lerman, a good friend and English Professor from ASU, and Tommy, my one and only friend from prison.

I only had one other good friend from prison besides Tommy. His name was Richard Stanley, and he overdosed and died back in 2004.

C'mon, man. I just got out. Let's get some heroin.

Not me. I don't mind having a couple of beers with you, but my dope-shooting days are over.

Booze
Beer

A few days after my graduation, we have a big party at Mom's house.

You Are Invited to Share in the Celebration of Matthew Parker's Graduation

With Live Music Performed by Billy Cioffi, Alex Holland & Walt Richardson

Besides family, many of my friends are there, both academics and musicians.

Billy, Alex, and Walt perform in my living room.

In June I get an email from Columbia, offering me a studio apartment on 113th Street, just a block from campus.

Dear Matthew Parker,

University Apartment Housing at Columbia is prepared to offer you a studio on 113th Street between Broadway and Amsterdam for $1,150, utilities not included. Please make payment by Saturday for first and last

I thought that I'd have room-mates because, Columbia said, few single apartments were available.

Hi. I'm majoring in alcohol consumption. How about you?

I was resigned to this. It was no worse than playing cellie roulette in prison, I figured.

Hi. I'm a major Holocaust denier. You?

But Columbia offers me my own apartment, and I can guess why.

This guy's an ex con. We better give him his own place. He may shank a roommate if he gets mad at him.

UAH-Off Campus

I'm willing to take advantage of this.

SPECIAL
BENIFITS
FOR
EX CONS

APPLICABLE
ANYWHERE

Chapter 9

I can never put my dick on hold.

> Are we gonna get some pussy tonight?

He's insistent, demanding, biologically determined.

> No.

> Oh come on. At least get me a blow job from a fat girl.

Constantly needing to be fondled, held, stroked, coddled, and, ideally, buried in a warm pussy.

> All right. Jerk me off then...

> ...preferably to a shaved beaver on the Internet.

He's worse than a woman.

> Does this bathing suit make me look small?

So no one is more dismayed than he when Nataly informs me that, despite her promise, she's still not prepared to have sex with me on my July visit.

> Whaddaya mean she ain't givin' up the pussy?

> We've been waiting since January for this.

But when she tells me why, my dick gets more excited.

> This sucks.

> She's a virgin? Holy mother of God.

It's just like a dick to want to fuck a virgin.

> After so many years in prison, why this?

> I think I'm going to faint.

My psyche and my dick have differing takes on taking Nataly's virginity.

> It would be so much nicer if she had a bit of experience.

> I can't wait to rip open that virgin cunt.

Dicks who want to fuck virgins are either perverts or sadists...

> You're a fool. It's no fun at all.

> Speak for yourself.

...or, more commonly, both.

There ain't nothing in the world like young, virgin pussy.

For us both, then, it's the worst possible scenario.

She's not young, just sexually immature.

A dick can dream, can't he?

But I love Nataly and am determined to make this relationship work.

You are not angry?

No. I was at first, but it's what's in our hearts that's important.

I get my fill of intimacy from her on this trip and leave satisfied with her promise that she'll be ready on my next visit in January.

I have trouble trusting men. But I know if you come back then your heart is probably in the right place.

Don't worry, mi amor. I'll be back. Now. Dame besos.

My dick, of course, is not happy at all.

I'm a little frightened of sex, so you must promise me that you'll be gentle.

Te prometo.

Christ. They sound like a fucking romance novel.

If it were up to him we'd be cheating on Nataly right now.

Hola, amor.

A real man would be out hunting for pussy right now. Just for spite.

But he can't be blamed completely: It's what he was made to do.

I am a fully functional love muscle designed to impregnate as many women as possible.

In essence, he's just greedy.

And, after 11 years in prison, what does he do with my freedom? Internet fucking porn.

If given free rein, most dicks would have harems of virgins waiting on them head and scrotum.

But my dick has very little say over my actions.

The Breast Implant

Bar & Grill

There's a titty bar. Stop. Let's go in. Wait. Oh please, let's go in.

GIRLS GIRLS GIRLS

OP

This is because I was surrounded by dicks in prison.

Prison dicks are greedy and paranoid and controlling and spend their lives spreading fear and hate.

Preserving the white race is essential to our continued existence.

The theory being that more money and more power would bring more pussy to their dicks.

I need to sell this stolen jewelry and buy more meth so I can get that stripper high, fuck her silly, and then pimp her out.

Which is what landed them in prison in the first place.

You're under arrest for being a complete dick.

Over the centuries, dicks have been nurtured by women to be less constantly dickish.

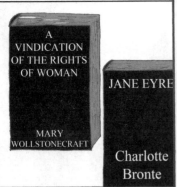

A VINDICATION OF THE RIGHTS OF WOMAN

MARY WOLLSTONECRAFT

JANE EYRE

Charlotte Bronte

Evolution has installed a built-in equalizer: If guys want to get laid, their dicks need to behave.

Were you looking at that bitch's tits?

No way, baby.

In sexual selection, females choose the males they prefer to mate with, which leads to all sorts of ridiculous behavior by males.

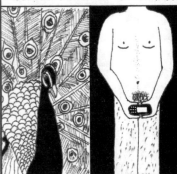

Dicks don't like not being selected.

I can't understand it. I sent her a picture of my dick.

Hmmm. Have you tried stalking?

But few women are choosing PRISON dicks.

No mail?

I wish I had a dirty woman to write to.

No. Me, too.

So their biggest fear is that women from their group might be selecting dicks from other, more colorful groups.

For this and other reasons, they deny the equality dictated by evolution...

It's an abomination for whites to interbreed with others.

...and have an uncanny ability to bring other dicks around to their cause.

Heil Hitler!

You bet.

As further proof of just what PRICKS Prison dicks really are, they love lesbians but hate gays.

It's an abomination for men to fuck men...

Unless, of course, they need a gay man to service their dicks.

...except when it's me doing the fucking.

After spending so many years locked up with these dicks, I find it a simple thing to control my dick because, in reality, he's just a dick.

How the fuck can you go months or even years at a time without getting laid?

I've learned from some stand-up mother fuckers.

I arrive in New York City on Tuesday, August 28, 2007.

Only to find out that my apartment isn't ready.

We're sorry, Mr. Parker, but your apartment is still being remodeled.

What?

Columbia puts me up in a tiny room with no TV or Internet access.

99 overpriced textbooks on the wall...

...99 overpriced texts...

Time Warner Cable was scheduled to hook up TV, phone, and Internet in my apartment on Thursday.

Yes. I need to reschedule my hook-up appointment

Sure. The soonest I can get someone back out there is in two weeks.

All my stuff is being delivered by UPS on Friday, and, as the apartment is unfurnished, I have a van rented for Saturday to drive to the New Jersey Ikea and buy all my furniture.

Newark International Airport

Jersey City

Manhattan

Statue of Liberty

Brooklyn

Ikea

For these reasons, I have to get into my apartment by Saturday at the latest.

Will my apartment be ready by Saturday?

Maybe. This is New York. This kind of thing happens all the time.

OFF CAMPUS HOUSING

I keep trying to find someone to bribe, but I guess I don't rate.

How 'bout I give you a hundred bucks?

This is New York. We don't take bribes.

OFF CAMPUS HOUSING

How far up the ladder do you have to be in this city before someone will take your bribe?

Can I see your boss, please?

No.

The city comptroller?

Don't be silly.

The fucking mayor?

Oh, please.

I sneak up to my apartment, and the workers there confirm my worst suspicions.

When do you think you guys will be done.

Maybe by Monday.

I then go to talk to my landlord, Dolores.

I need to be in my apartment by Saturday.

It's very unlikely it will be done that soon.

But I can't cancel the rental van, and classes start on Monday.

Nothing I can do.

Dolores is once removed from the bureaucracy, so railing at her would not have helped. I try to bribe her, but she won't take it.

How about I give you some money to help speed things up?

Money is not the issue here.

My last trump is to appeal to her working-class status.

Look. I'm not one of these Ivy League rich kids. I worked my ass off to get here.

So have I.

Something in her softens.

You just show up here at one o'clock on Saturday, and I'll have your keys for you.

506

I learned later that she and her crew had stayed until 10:30 on Friday night to make sure it was ready and had also moved my five or six very large boxes from UPS up to my fourth-floor apartment.

As a child, I had always wanted to be a fighter pilot.

I knew all about Chuck Yeager long before "The Right Stuff."

My fighter pilot dream was torched when I witnessed military jets spraying napalm on villages in Vietnam, but I never lost my love of military aircraft.

Boron was located next to Edwards Air Force Base, where Yeager first broke the sound barrier in 1947.

Built on a mountain, the prison camp was an old Army Air Force barracks.

Higher up the mountain were the education, industries, and maintenance buildings, along with, at its highest point, a radar tower.

The air was alive with the roar of military jets and window-rattling sonic booms.

kABOOM!

One afternoon I was standing on the lookout, just north of the radar tower, when right in front of me a B-1 bomber, its variable wings swept back, flew right by me.

It was cruising at about eye level with me, banking to the northwest, and I could see a pilot clearly in the cockpit.

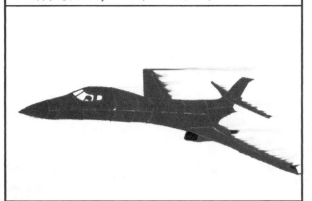

It was a quiet plane, so quiet that I heard the chase planes, a couple of T-38s, before I heard the bomber.

Painted primer black, it was huge and moving fast — a beautiful machine, the ultimate symbol of freedom to me.

It was simply the freedom of flight, and I was much more envious of it than of all those goofy gulls back at TI.

Speed is just distance divided by time. By comparison, I was a slow-moving creature, my distances restricted, my time slowed.

In that plane I could be thousands of miles from Boron in just a few hours and blow the living fuck out of anyone trying to catch me.

The B-1 was everything I was not, yet it somehow sparked a measure of hope in my incarcerated heart.

My first job at Boron was raking lines in the dirt.

This menial job was incorporated on every prison yard I've ever been on.

YARD CREW

or, more colloquially:

Rake and Bake (summer)
Rake and Shake (winter)
Raking Rocks
Raking Dirt
Dirt & Rock Technicians
Linesmen

To break up the monotony, I'd sometimes do CROP circles, which often angered the guards.

Rake straight lines, damn it.

After a few days, I was assigned to the print shop, where I learned how to silkscreen.

THE DOORS

Later I applied for and got a job as a carpenter/handyman.

Most everyone worked at Boron, and indeed on every prison yard I've ever been on.

FPC Boron Work Crews

Hinkley Crew
☰ ☰ ☰ ☰☰☰

Edwards AFB Crew
☰ ☰ ☰ ☰☰☰

UNICOR
☰ ☰ ☰ ☰

Construction/Maintenance
☰☰

Dorm Porters
☰ ☰ ☰ ☰

Yard Crew
☰

I was also given a chance to get my high school diploma.

Would you like to get your GED?

No.

But we'll put $25 on your books if you pass.

Sign me up.

Classes begin...

But you haven't been in school in 11 years, and...

Whoa. Who said anything about classes?

You just give me the test.

True to my word, I took the test and passed with no problem.

General Equivalency
of the State of California

This Certifies that
Matthew Parker
has met the requirements to be awarded a high school equivalency

Diploma

Awarded this **18** day of May, 1988,
by the City of Sacramento, State of California

I learned very quickly not to make too many friends in jail or prison.

My name's Wizard.

They call me snake.

Just when I got close to somebody, they'd move me or him.

Let's go, Parker. You're rolling up.

No No NO.

Plus it was hard to weed out the normal guys from the sex offenders, rats, and the more blatant racists.

I just found a friend whose sexual proclivities fall within the standard norms and who's neither a snitch nor a pawn to agents of intolerance.

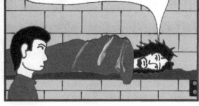

I made lots of acquaintances, but few real friends.

They call me the reaper.

That's nice. But is there just a simple "Joe" around here?

I was put in the biker dorm upon my arrival at Boron.

Up the hill, last dorm on your right.

The only problem here was that bikers, especially gang members, had little use for junkies.

Anybody weak enough to be a junkie...

...is weak enough to snitch.

After checking my paperwork, they tolerated my presence, but we had little in common.

UNITED STATES
DISTRICT COURT
District of Arizona - Phoenix

Parker, Matthew J
DOB 04/05/1960
BOP No. 19972-008
FBI No. 548904CA5
U.S. Bureau of Prisons
Federal sentencing guidlines:
0 - 10 months
Sentence: two years

Checking the paperwork of new guys was standard practice. At Boron, a prisoner worked in admin., where he could sneak a peek into your jacket, but in most instances they'd simply demand to see it the moment you arrived.

Your court papers.

Quickly.

My only real friend was a coworker and fellow carpenter who went by the nickname Heek.

And how do I know that you're not a snitch?

Because they checked my paperwork, too.

Panel 1:
After a few months, I was offered a job at FCI Phoenix.

"Do you want to go back to Phoenix, Parker?"

BOP STATEMENT OF PURPOSE

Panel 2:
They were building a women's FPC there and were looking for guys from that area with construction skills.

WANTED

Slave laborers who want to be transferred to FCI Phoenix

Help contribute to the profitable delinquency of the prison complex.

All interested parties please contact your counselors.

Panel 3:
I volunteered for the transfer.

"Sure. I'll be closer to home, and I even know a blonde who might visit me."

BOP STATEMENT OF PURPOSE

Panel 4:
My friend Heek warned me not to go.

"This is like the military. Never volunteer for anything. And why give up all this freedom, anyway?"

Panel 5:
Rumor had it that we would be housed in trailers, off the main yard.

"They're not gonna put us on the yard. They won't mix minimum and medium security prisoners."

"They can do whatever the fuck they want. And Christ, you'll be building a prison for them."

Panel 6:
A few weeks after I volunteered, some Mexicans planned a liquor run.

"They literally run to Boron between counts and buy half gallons of vodka."

"You're kidding?"

"Nope. Try that at FCI Phoenix."

Panel 7:
Heek and I chipped in 15 dollars in dimes and nickels for our share and got blissfully drunk, along with half the yard.

"Now this is a proper send-off, Parker."

"Just like real life."

"Oh when the swallows come back to Capistrano..."

We were transferred to FCI Phoenix in June of 1988.

All of you guys will be housed in Pima-B.

There were no trailers. Instead, we were housed on the yard with all the medium security prisoners.

What are you guys in for?

Bank robbery.

FCI Phoenix was a two-man-per-cell yard.

Who's your new cellie?

Some asshole.

The problem was to find someone compatible to cell up with...

Bummer, dude.

Well, I found a guy to live with...

... and then get the administrators to move you.

...but they told me it'll be a month or two wait.

It was also a controlled-movement yard, which meant we had a lot less freedom than we enjoyed at Boron.

Time to go. The yard closes at 8:30 here.

Fuck. It was open until midnight at Boron.

And the food, although gourmet when compared to the county, didn't measure up to Boron's.

Where's the baked potato bar?

The plus side was that, because it was such a big prison, there were a lot more activities.

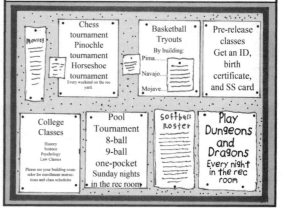

We were minimum security inmates on a medium security yard.

Bureau of Prisons Custody Levels

1 - 2: Minimum security: At this level, community custody, or out custody, can be obtained. Housed in Federal Prison Camps (FPCs).

3 - 4: Medium security: Housed in Federal Correctional Institutions (FCIs).

5 - 6: Maximum security. Housed in United States Penitentiaries (USPs)

And as such, we were allowed to work outside the double-fence perimeter.

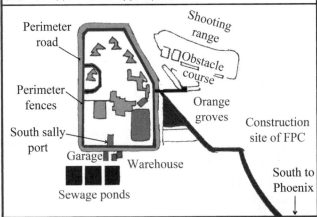

The day after we arrived, they took us out the south sally port and had us hoeing weeds in an orange grove in 110-degree heat.

They hadn't even broken ground yet on the prison we were brought there to help build.

After two days of baking out there I applied for and got a job as a mechanic.

U.S. Bureau of Prisons
Federal Correctional Institution - Phoenix

Employment Memo

Experienced mechanic wanted for maintenance work on official prison vehicles. Applicants must have community custody and be familiar with all phases of conventional and diesel mechanics. Pay starts at 65 cents an hour.

FCI Phoenix had no guard towers but instead used Chevy trucks to patrol the perimeter.

My job was to keep these trucks and other prison vehicles running.

I basically sat around the air-conditioned garage for eight hours a day, listening to the radio while waiting for the trucks to break down.

Music was still a big part of my survival. So I was pleasantly surprised when, that summer, Walt Richardson and the Morning Star Band performed on the yard.

And of course I had a Walkman.

At Boron, a DJ named Uncle Joe at KLOS did the Seventh Day every Sunday night, when he played seven of rock's greatest albums in a row.

This is Uncle Joe Benson, and you are listening to KLOS, Los Angeles.

I would lie in my bunk listening for hours...

...and when I sent him a letter, he did indeed play my seven albums.

	Dear Uncle Joe,
	Please play the following five albums (two doubles) for my incarcerated ass.
Double	Deep Purple - Made in Japan
Double	Pink Floyd - the Wall
	The Beatles - Abbey Road
	Led Zeppelin - III
	Elton John - Madman across the Water

At FCI Phoenix, I could pick up all the local stations.

You're rockin' 93.3, KDKB.

The feds had TV rooms. We were not allowed to have TVs in our cells.

Showtime

So I spent a lot of time listening to music.

Hey, Matt, there's a good movie on.

No thanks. I'm gonna stay in here and jam.

I'm just as wary about making friends at Columbia as I was at Boron.

I never fit in at prison, and I certainly don't fit in here.

School of the Arts

Orientation

At ASU, this wasn't a problem.

But Columbia's writing program is made up of tight-knit little groups.

First-Year Writing Students Read Your Work At the Ding Dong Reading Series

The classes are small, and the second-year writing students snub us first-years.

Hi. I'd like to read at one of your events.

Sorry. We're all full for the semester.

But I thought it was designed for first-years?

Sorry. We're all full for the semester.

I feel like a new fish on the yard.

One of the first people I meet is a second-year non-fiction girl from Afghanistan.

You don't have any Afghan opium on you, do you?

Sorry, no. I left it in my other back pack.

Prime

Her name is Murwarid, and she's a departmental research assistant, or DRA.

Well, I'll expect some next time we meet. Not much, just a bushel or two.

Prime

I also meet Dan, a hard-drinking fiction writer from Vermont.

What's up, man? C'mon over here and have a beer.

Thank you. I believe I will.

He and Murwarid are the only second-years who're decent to me, at least at first.

When the swallows come back to Capistrano...

180

Once classes begin, I'm puzzled by the way people communicate.

I'm going into class now. I'll call you the minute I get out.

Everyone has iPods and cell phones; everyone sends text messages; everyone is on Facebook and/or Myspace and is heavily into social networking.

Ok. Then, he said to me, "A poet in a dive like..." oops. There's my other line. Text you later.

The writing division of the School of the Arts at Columbia is a small community, with 90 percent of them in their 20s.

So, like, he didn't respond to my friend request, and this after I sexted him...

It was easy to lose myself in the maze of Arizona State University, but Columbia is another matter.

There's only about 70 of you first-years.

Christ. There was like 3,000 in my graduating class at ASU.

Some of my fellow students encourage me to join Facebook and to send them text messages, but I can't bring myself to do either.

You need to get on Facebook.

No thanks. As social animals go, I'm not much of one.

I just don't get the "What are you doing now?" scene.

Right this minute? I'm looking at a website called Teens in Tokyo.

Prisons are very crowded, to the point where privacy doesn't exist at all.

Now that I'm out, I crave solitude and just about give a rat's ass what God is doing at this moment, let alone anyone else.

You have a collect text from Jesus. Do you accept the charges?

No. Tell him to call on Africa.

There's also a rift between the disciplines in the writing division at Columbia's School of the Arts. I call them the genre gangs.

Nonfiction   Fiction   Poetry

They remind me of prison gangs.

Aryan Brotherhood   Black Guerrilla Family   Mexican Mafia

The inter-genre resentment isn't as thick as it was in prison but is there nonetheless.

I seldom cross genres.

I don't even talk to fiction folks.

I stick with my own.

This is especially true in the way the second-year students treat us first-years.

Not only is he nonfiction, but a first-year, to boot.

I find this out when I try to read at the events controlled by second-years.

I would like to read my work at one of your events.

Fine. Send me an email.

I've sent you emails.

I'll check my inbox.

I'm effectively held out by the second-years.

I'm a subaltern. I have no agency.

On Halloween night, the School of the Arts hires a party boat to sail around the city while serving free food and drinks.

I go by myself to see Zappa plays Zappa at the Beacon Theatre instead.

But I'm used to being a loner.

All writers are loners, Parker.

Is that so?

Nor am I completely alienated. I go bar-hopping with Dan a lot.

Sure it is. Just as all writers can be the worst kind of assholes.

23 AVE B.   646-6

After a while under his second-year wing, Dan's friends begin to accept me.

Parker, these are my asshole friends.

Hi

They all hang out in this filthy bar on Amsterdam Avenue, typically close to campus.

Of course, I use the word "Writer" loosely.

I know what you mean.

It's such a dive it doesn't even have a name but instead goes by its street number.

1020

The bathrooms are so reminiscent of those in the Horseshoe at the Madison Street Jail that I refuse to return to the bar after a few visits.

Did you know that the ratio for failure in rehab is about the same as it is for MFAs?

Is that a fact?

I was an outsider in Prison and am an outsider at Columbia.

I prefer standing outside of groups and looking in.

Me, too.

Let's get the fuck out of here.

No shit.

183

Chapter 10

In prison, I was an outsider because I wasn't a racist. I could only be an insider within the narrow confines of my own race.

> **Hey? New guy?**
>
> **Come on over and join the master race.**
>
> **Yes?**
>
> **No thanks.**

The one group I fell into by default— white boys—I wanted no part of.

> **But you're an automatic member by virtue of your pure white skin.**
>
> **I know. But I think I'll just do my time and go home.**

I wanted nothing to do with the majority of white boys I'd met in jail and prison.

> **Is that mongoloid Mexican here to see you?**
>
> **Yes. I'm selling him art.**

But I had to abide by white boy rules, like never offering a person of color a seat on my bed.

> **Hi. Can I sit down?**
>
> **Sorry, no. Now, I have these birthday cards...**

I didn't feel too bad about it because it wasn't like people of color didn't have racial issues of their own.

> **Stupid gringo.**

Every race was encouraged to hate every other race in prison, to the point where violence was always on the verge of breaking out.

> **Stupid Mexicans.**
>
> **Stupid Muslims.**
>
> **Stupid people of indeterminate race.**

Indeed, the only ones preventing an all-out racial war were the guys in charge.

> **We want to go to war with the stupid Mexicans.**
>
> **No way, men. Race riots are bad for business.**

Another factor was that the frequency of violence was directly proportional to security levels.

Arizona Department of Corrections
Security Classification Levels*

1 - 2: Minimum Security

3 - 4: Medium Security

5 - 6: Maximum Security

*Inmate reclassification occurs every six months.

On minimum yards, most everyone was within four years of going home, and many had worked their way to a minimum yard from higher security levels.

I did 10 years on a medium yard and got 2 to the gate. I ain't fucking that up for no damn race riot.

Plus, everybody works on minimum yards, which in itself relieves tension.

We need to go and beat down that youngster in dorm three.

Fuck that. I'm too damn tired.

On medium and maximum security yards, most guys are doing hard time. Men with decades left to serve have a lot less to lose.

I got 20 years to my first parole board, so I'll stick anyone you guys want me to.

But excessive violence like stabbings and race riots were rare even on the medium yards I did time on because everything from individual shankings to all-out war must be sanctioned by gang leaders.

Calm down. We ain't stabbing nobody. We just need someone to do beat-downs on guys in debt to us, nothing more.

Although on occasion a rogue prisoner stabbed another, causing the administrators to lock down the yard and do a cell-to-cell search, which in turn shut down most of the extortion, gambling, and drug rackets.

Attention! This is a house-to-house shakedown. Everyone strip to your boxers and line up against this wall.

So most disagreements between prisoners were settled with one-on-one fights, which were governed by strict codes of conduct.

OK, you two. This is a simple fight. No weapons, none of your buddies jumping in, and it's over when one of yous yields.

Another way to avoid violence in prison was to be prepared, at all times, for violence.

That dude's talkin' shit about you.

What dude?

I sidestepped many a fight by showing that I wasn't afraid to fight.

You got something to say, say it to my face, mother fucker.

This was sometimes referred to as a heart check. I'm not a big guy, but stature in prison is often measured by your heart, which in turn is measured by an apparent lack of fear.

Dude, you don't wanna get into it with me.

Fuck you. You got a problem, let's handle it.

If, for any reason, a fight is called for and you refuse to step up, you'd be gang beaten by members of your own race and run off the yard.

There's a guy in dorm six got called a punk and he won't fight. What should we do?

Send a crew to beat him down and roll him up into protective custody.

There's also the respect factor. In prison you never know who you're fucking with. My ADOC number is 87078. It never changes. As years went by and issued ADOC numbers got higher and higher, I was treated with more respect because my number was older.

That dude with the old number. He's not down with the cause?

No. He's on an independent, but he don't bother no one. Shoots a little dope on weekends and always pays his bills on time.

And, as an independent, I was outside of the direct control of gang leaders. Independents with years already served are the ones most likely to shove a shank up your ass with little or no provocation.

I'm gonna fight that old geezer in the laundry room.

Don't fuck with that old-timer.

The simple fact is that anyone can shank anyone at anytime, and there isn't a goddamn thing the administrators or the gang leaders can do about it.

Someone got shanked in the laundry room.

Shit. There goes the weekend.

This was certainly not the case with me. I never carried a shank. But of course no one knew this.

Think that old-timer is packing?

Don't know and don't wanna find out.

In 2000, I got into it with a young-ster on the medium security Win-chester yard in Tucson.

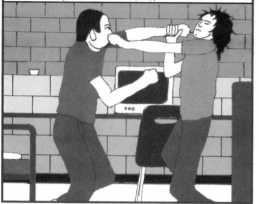

It started out as simple horseplay but ballooned into a fight in which he split my head open with a lock and got in trouble for it with the head white boy.

That was fucked up what he did, using a weapon on a fellow peckerwood. You get healed up and you'll get an-other crack at him.

I never did get another crack at him, because he PCed up soon after.

I need to get off the yard.

Don't tell me. You owe money for drugs, right?

yes.

Come with me.

YARD OFFICE

This is another way to avoid violence—all you need to do is tell the guards that your life is in danger and they'll move you off the yard.

So you want to check in? Well, if you was to give us some names, we might help you.

PC is short for protective custody, or punk city.

Will you put me in PC?

For now. Later we'll move you to another yard.

There was another guy on the medium security Santa Cruz yard at Perryville who had stabbed himself when I was there in 1992. This was known as a PC move.

Help. The niggers stabbed me.

Wizard, come quick. Ivan got stuck.

His move came close to starting an all-out war between the whites and the blacks, but it turned out he owed a lot of money for drugs and thought that his trick would get him off the yard with nobody the wiser.

I can't believe that idiot stabbed himself.

What better way to get off the yard?

And it almost worked, too.

But by far the best way to avoid violence in prison was to stay out of the mix.

Most assaults occur because of drug or gambling debts.

Drugs were available, but they were expensive—up to 10 times their street value.

All deals were done on a credit basis, and going into debt was considered a grave weakness.

I used in prison, but only rarely, mostly on weekends.

This was because the majority of contraband came through visitation.

I was also disciplined enough to buy my heroin only after I had my creature comforts.

It's almost impossible to be a junkie in prison anyway; to have both the everyday availability of heroin and the money to afford it.

Rather, prison was like a prolonged detox, where I got clean for a couple years before going on another dope-fueled street binge.

The reason we always seem to have trouble fitting in is a direct result of group selection.

If we all hate darkies together...

...then our kids will all hate darkies...

...together.

RED Neck

People are more comfortable in groups of people who think the same way they do.

Those stupid conservatives.

Those stupid liberals.

It's very tribal.

Stupid south tribe.

Stupid north tribe.

Thus white boys are naturally more comfortable with other white boys in a prison atmosphere, particularly when our propensity to clique up is nurtured.

Stupid Jews niggers, spics, chinks, queers.

Yeah. Yous ain't as smart as us pekawuhds.

Just as poets feel more accepted with other poets at Columbia...

Stupid fiction writers.

Stupid nonfiction writers.

...and second-years with other second-years.

Stupid first-years.

But it doesn't have to be this way.

Stupid literary Darwinists.

Stupid literary theorists.

Being aware of the machinations of evolution makes it easier to escape its many traps.

Stupid nature.

Stupid nurture.

We usurp the designs of our selfish genes, after all, every time we use something as simple as birth control.

I forgot to take my stupid pill and I'm pregnant again.

Stupid bitch.

I can't afford to go home for Thanksgiving during my first semester at Columbia, so my fiction friend Stephen bakes a turkey at his apartment.

Never cooked a turkey before, but I guess it ain't much different from a chicken.

It smells delicious.

He's from Ireland, where they don't celebrate Thanksgiving.

May I offer a toast to give thanks?

A modest proposal, mate.

Joining us is another fiction writer, Roberto, from Brazil, where they also don't celebrate Thanksgiving.

Roberto, have a sip of this Irish whiskey. I even got teetotaling Matty to do a shot.

Don't mind if I do.

I'm touched by their kindness to share this meal with me.

So tell us about this holiday of yours, mate. What's its story?

And it sure beats Thanksgiving in jail or prison.

Wish we could fly away for Turkey Day.

Turkeys can't fly, rope dick.

I fly home for Christmas, and we all meet at my sister's for a huge dinner.

I also visit Billy and Gwen.

Welcome home.

Billy and I have been talking on the phone three or four times a week since I left, mostly about politics.

Tolerance is not a popularity contest. Rights are inherent no matter how many people disagree.

No shit. We've had to fight for every inch of basic civil rights since the Civil War.

But it's good to see him again. And to hear him.

Take a load for free,

I also visit other friends.

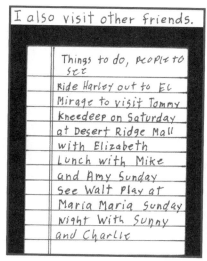

Things to do, PEOPLE TO SEE
Ride Harley out to El Mirage to visit Tommy
kneedeep on Saturday at Desert Ridge Mall with Elizabeth
Lunch with Mike and Amy Sunday
See Walt play at Maria Maria Sunday Night with Sunny and Charlie

I then fly to Cartagena for my January visit with Nataly.

We had decided to spend a week on the beach, so I fly her up from Cali.

CARTAGENA

VENEZUELA

MEDELLIN

★ BOGOTÁ

CALI

ECUADOR

BRAZIL

And it's in that romantic, Colombian city where we try for amor completo.

It is indeed painful for her.

Gently, amor. Gently.

I'm being gentle.

This is mostly because the act itself frightens her.

Lo siento.

Christ. It's like I'm dating a fucking teenager.

She views sex as an obligation and fights it every step of the way, which of course only increases her anxiety, along with my frustration.

I'm trying to please you.

It's not just about me. It's about us. Both of us together.

And my dick is not happy at all.

Whose bright idea was it to fuck a virgin? Christ, what a pain.

But we are convinced that our love will overcome this, and that, in the future, she'll be able to enjoy sex as much as me.

Maybe it is, as you say, an act of love.

Mutual love. ¿Entiendes? Amor para nosotros.

I was released from FCI Phoenix in January of 1989, three months early, to a halfway house.

Here's your release papers. Your taxi will be here soon.

None other than Behavioral Systems Southwest.

I was not in the spoon by noon my first day out...

When can I get out of here to, uh, look for work?

Not until tomorrow.

... but was by my second.

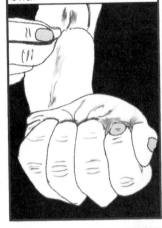

Finding work was difficult without a car, but I managed to get a job as a mechanic in a garage close to the halfway house.

The job don't pay shit, but we really need the help.

I'll take it.

I changed out transmissions.

But I was using every day, so it was only a matter of time.

Your last UA came back dirty, Parker.

To tell you the truth, I really don't give a fuck.

Within three weeks I violated and was put back on the yard at FCI Phoenix.

Due to the BOPs Zero-tolerance approach, you're under arrest for a dirty urine sample.

I can give you another one, if you'd like.

It was like I never left, except I had to buy everything all over again.

FCI-PHOENIX
Commissary List

Soap.........................____
Soap dish.................____
Razors.....................____
Shampoo..................____
Deodorant................____
Toothpaste...............____
Toothbrush...............____
Nonfilter cigarettes......____
Walkman..................____

I was razzed by my friends for violating my parole so quickly, but I looked at it as more of a vacation...

What? Did you just drop in to do your laundry?

Couldn't even stay out for a month?

...or an extended furlough.

Ha ha. Very funny. But at least I got high and lapped up some pussy.

I could not admit to myself that I was living my life like an asshole.

Once a junkie, always a junkie. Is that it?

Hell no. I'll stop shooting dope when I'm good and ready.

And of course Mom was upset.

Collect call from the Federal Correctional Institution, Phoenix. Do you accept the charges?

Yes. You fuck.

But I only had a couple months left on my sentence until my mandatory release.

Can I get my old job back?

No. You lost your out custody for violating your parole.

Guess I'll just take rocks, then.

OFFICE HOURS

Mon - Fri 9:00 - 3:00
Saturday 11:00 - 2:00
Closed Sundays and Holidays.
For emerg____ please contact the ____ ____fice

On April 19, 1989, my sentence was effectively terminated.

So how does parole work when I get out this time?

You're technically on parole until your sentence expires in late August.

No more peeing in a cup. No more AA or NA meetings.

I'll never piss in a cup for a cop again.

Never say never.

I was, once again, a completely free man.

Free to shoot all the dope I want.

Be careful. Your body is clean, so you're much more likely to overdose.

I was in the spoon by noon on the day of my release.

Could you pass me that syringe, please?

Sure.

Thank you.

You're welcome.

And was strung out within a month.

I need a front. 20 black. I'm sick.

Pinche puto. You pay me later or no más. Comprende?

But I did try to do the right thing, at least at first.

I got a job, Ma. Get off my case.

A shitty job. You'd better get your ass together, sonny boy.

Sarah and I got back together.

And I enrolled in Scottsdale Community College the following fall, majoring in journalism...

You need to buy books with that money.

I need to get high. I'll hustle the money for books later on.

STUDE
CENTER

H
M
CL

... but dropped out two weeks later.

That was short and sweet. Now what?

We return the few books that I actually bought for dope money.

I picked up a possession charge in July of 1990.

Well, look what we found on the ground behind you.

Bullshit. We saw you drop it as we pulled up.

That's not mine.

I was released from the Horseshoe on OR, and the charge was later dismissed without prejudice.

You realize that a dismissal means the state can refile these charges anytime within the next seven years with little or no warning?

I realized a long time ago that the state can do pretty much whatever the hell it wants.

194

In October I was busted for shoplifting and charged with burglary.

Burglary? Are you fucking kidding me?

So?

You had no money on you. This proves that you went into the store with the intent to steal.

This was simply a way of enhancing what should've been a misdemeanor shoplifting into a felony burglary.

It doesn't prove anything. Maybe I just went in there to take a piss.

It proves intent. You can argue out the particulars in court.

Intent is, apparently, everything.

And it's a fucking felony?

Class four, carrying a maximum sentence of 3.75 years.

They took me directly to the Horseshoe.

This sucks.

Well, now you know not to boost with no money on you.

Sarah had been waiting for me in the car. Parked illegally just a few steps from the store's exit.

She watched them bust me.

Watched the store detectives cuff me up and lead me back into the store before she drove away.

Drove back to whatever it was that she did to score drugs on her own.

I had been boosting a long time to support my habit, usually jeans. Levis 501s. And cigarettes. I could always fence jeans and cigarettes.

How much for all this?

Ten bucks each for the pants, a buck a pack for the smokes.

The problem was I had to do it every day, two or three times a day. The odds were all wrong. Sooner or later, I'd be caught.

Where we going?

But you've hit that Mervyn's four times this week.

Mervyn's in Paradise Valley.

You got a better idea?

I knew this every time I walked into a store.

Be careful, baby.

I'll be careful. You just keep your eyes open.

I would go into a store and pick up four or five pairs of jeans, then tuck them under an arm and walk out.

It was important not to conceal them. If I concealed them, they could nab me in the store.

I walked, quickly. They had to catch me outside the door, but Sarah was watching: parked illegally mere feet from the door.

If anyone suspicious was lurking out there, she'd drive the car away. If the car was gone, I knew it wasn't safe.

The day I got caught the car was there, so I thought it was safe, but Sarah hadn't been paying attention.

OCTOBER 1990

SU	MO	TU	WE	TH	FR	SU
	1	2	3	4	5	6
7	8	9				

They refiled the posses-
sion charge in November.

Parker, step out of the Pod with your ID.

What's up?

Page two.

Mom bonded me out for Christmas.

His bond is $500, cash only.

In February, just six weeks later, Sarah and I were in a dope house around 15th Avenue and Grand and got caught up in a raid.

McDowell Rd.

10

🏠 Dope house

19th Ave.

Grand Ave.

15th Ave.

Van Buren

I was in the process of trad-
ing jeans for heroin when they kicked in the door, guns blazing.

POLICE OFFICERS! SEARCH WARRANT! NOBODY MOVE!

POLICE

I had a syringe in my pocket, so was arrested for possession of drug paraphernalia.

Well, what have we here?

Sarah was let go with-
out even being searched.

You can go now, miss.

They held me without bond because I was already out on bond.

The charge is drug paraphernalia. No bond. Next.

Kicking for three days in the Horseshoe was the same as it ever was.

I was housed in Madison, but after having a cell for just two days, they mysteriously released me.

Why they letting me go, Sarge?

Don't know. Says here only that the charges were dropped.

The next day, Sarah and I were in the same neighborhood.

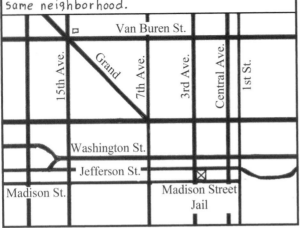

We had just fixed and were walking up Grand close to 15th Avenue, when one of the cops who had busted me six days earlier happened to drive by.

Spotting me, he stopped us, thinking I had escaped.

I just busted you. You had no bond. How the hell did you get out?

This was an easy probable cause for stopping me.

I don't know. They just released me.

You sure you didn't escape? I better check it out.

He ran my name and found I had a warrant out for my arrest.

Parker, Matthew J. Maricopa County warrant for drug paraphernalia. Issued yesterday; 1-30-1991.

It seems they didn't file the Paraphernalia charge in time, which is why I'd been released the previous day.

This the booking officer? Yes. I have one kick-out: Parker, Matthew J.

Ok, we'll cut him loose.

After my release, they refiled the charge.

In the Superior Court
of Arizona in and for the
County of Maricopa
Arrest Warrant issued for:
Parker, Matthew Joseph
DOB: 04/05/1960
POB: Bridgeport, CT
Charge(s): Possession of drug
paraphernalia
Date of arrest: 01/24/1991
Date of refile: 01/29/1991
Pending Charges: 3rd degree
burglary, Release $500 bond
POND (posession of a narcotic
drug), Release O.R.

I was re-arrested and taken back to county jail.

I've never been through the Horseshoe before.

Oh yeah? Well this is my second time in a fucking week.

Chapter 11

In my first semester at Columbia, I couldn't get a work-study job, although not for lack of trying.

Find a job yet, Matty?

Fuck no, Stephen.

I had suspicions that my past was the reason.

Why d'you think that is?

They're overly cautious. Why hire a felon when you don't have to?

In red-state Arizona, I can't even vote, but I was able to get a work-study job easily.

You should know I'm a convicted...

You're hired.

But in blue-state New York, Columbia ignored my applications—hoping, no doubt, that I'd find work elsewhere.

Work-Study Position: American Studies
Administrative Asst: III (Class III/#0877)
Work-Study Position: Social Justice
Work-Study Position: America Reads
Work-Study Job: Admissions/Arts
Work-Study Job: Butler Library

I used to rage at prison bureaucracy while ignoring the fact that it was my own actions that put me there.

You're under arrest.

Fuck you. If drugs were legal, you wouldn't even have a job.

And it was these same actions, committed many years in my past, that allowed Columbia to push me around now.

But drugs aren't legal, are they?

No.

At first I was furious at Columbia's bureaucracy, blaming them for my past.

These fuckers don't believe in rehabilitation.

I think it's more that they don't believe in taking any chances.

Just like I blamed my high school administrators for my failure in fulfilling my dream of attending college.

You wanted to see me?

Fuck you. I'll just quit.

You're being suspended for smoking on school grounds.

Quit what? Smoking? Or school?

Someone does eventually take a chance on me: the Law School.

Columbia Law School Is Hiring Proctors

Columbia Law is hiring individuals to proctor the final exams of our law students. The job pays $12 an hour for regular proctors ($15 for head proctors). All those interested must attend a training session in Jerome Green Hall (GRHL) 107. Dates to be announced in

I find a pleasant irony in this...

Hi. I'm here to apply for the exam proctor position.

...not least of which is the fact that the only people at Columbia who will hire the convicted felon are at the law school.

Can you read? / Yes.

You're hired.

This is probably because I don't tell them I'm a convicted felon when they don't ask.

Just fill out the electronic application form and email it back to me. There are no trick questions.

Thank You.

Although surely my secret is out. I'll tell anyone about my past, even if they just hint at it slightly.

So? What did you do before you came to New York?

Well, first I did a lot of illegal shit. Then I became a junkie. Then I went to prison a bunch of times...

The job consists of basically being a guard.

An ex con assigned the task of making sure future Ivy League lawyers don't cheat on their exams.

Keep your eyes on your own computer screen, please.

It's a decent paying gig, though sporadic.

How's the new job?

Pretty cool, but I only work at finals time, with a few midterms thrown in here and there.

Later I apply for a departmental research assistant (DRA) position.

The School of the Arts is now hiring departmental research assistants (DRAs).

Duties include hosting events, several hours a week of office work, which will include, but is not limited to, making copies, sending emails, composing letters and announcements, and answering the phone.

I'm interviewed by two venerable fiction writers/professors and their aides.

Good afternoon, Mr. Parker.

Hello. Mr. Parker.

Take a seat, Mr. Parker.

The interview is so solemn and serious that it feels like I'm back in prison facing a parole board.

In all the times I've been to prison, I only went to one parole board.

PAROLE HISTORY

Parker, Matthew J.
FBI No.: 548904CA5
BOP No.: 19972-008
1988: Hearing waived by inmate
ADOC No.: 87078
1992: Hearing waived by inmate
1993: Paroled from ASPC Perryville
1997: Truth in sentencing, parole
    not available
2001: Truth in sentencing, parole
    not available

It was on my third sentence, when I was in Perryville State Prison, west of Phoenix, in the summer of 1993.

Good afternoon, Mr. Parker.

Hello, Mr. Parker.

Take a seat, Mr. Parker.

I went to the board after serving about half of a 4.5-year sentence.

Parole board hearing for Parker, Matthew J. # 87078
Type of hearing: Home Arrest
Sentence A: 3rd degree burglary, 2 years, to run concurrent with B and C.
Sentence B: Possession of a narcotic drug, 2 years, to run concurrent with A and C.
Sentence C: Possession of drug paraphernalia, 1.75 years, to run concurrent with A and B.
Sentence D: Attempted possession of a narcotic drug, 2.5 years, to run consecutive with A, B, and C.

But even though it was my first parole board, I wasn't surprised by the completely inane questions they asked.

Why do you think you deserve to be paroled, Mr. Parker?

I mean, how was I supposed to answer that, considering I was in for "attempted" possession of heroin?

Well, given the incomparable serious nature of my crime along with the innumerable victims I've hurt with my immoral and indecent acts throughout the state, I really don't think that parole would be appropriate at this time.

At the DRA interview, they ask me equally inane questions.

What would you do to improve how the events here are run?

The events in question are creative writing lectures with some pretty famous writers, along with student readings and other get-togethers.

Columbia's School of the Arts Presents
The Creative Writing Lectures
Coming in Spring, 2008

Kathryn Harrison: 7pm, March 12th, Dodge 413

George Saunders: 7pm, April 17th, Philosophy 301

DRA duties at these events are to set up tables and lay out wine and cheese, then clean up afterward.

This apparently required a major catering intellect.

No. The cheese needs to be placed approximately seven centimeters from the wine.

The reward for being hired is a minor stipend and about 16 grand taken off a year's tuition.

How much to do what? I never had such a lame job even in prison.

It will help me immensely, and not just financially. All the DRAs hired got first choice of workshop professors.

COLUMBIA UNIVERSITY
School of the Arts

Class Preference Form

Nonfiction Workshop
First choice Locke
Second choice O'Toole
Third choice Scammell

The questions continue:

What would you tell a prospective student about the School of the Arts if they asked you about it?

What? The writing division?

I don't believe it's possible to nod condescendingly, but this is what I remember them doing.

Well, I certainly wouldn't tell them how much it cost.

It was the same shit at my parole board.

What would you do if you made parole today?

I answered truthfully. I'd had it with the whole rehab scene.

Well, I'll tell you what I won't do. I won't go to NA meetings, or AA meetings, or any of that other crap.

To my lasting astonishment, I was granted Parole.

We admire your honesty.

The DRA parole board, on the other hand...

We'll get back to you.

Acing the interview wouldn't have mattered.

Well, I would explain the manifold diversity which makes the School of the Arts such an unfettered joy to attend—at the right price, too.

Did they really want their highbrow events staffed by a tattoed ex con?

"Essay as Hack"

And this one I got at the state prison in Florence, Arizona.

203

From the Horseshoe they took me to the Towers.

Let's go, Parker. Your ride is here.

For a while Sarah was visiting as much as possible.

Hey, baby.

Hey.

NO kissing Allowed

She was living at Mom's and taking the bus down to visit

Whatcha been doing?

Not much. Waiting for my income tax check.

NO kissing Allowed

We even discussed marriage.

We can get married right here in the visitation room.

That would be great.

Being locked up, I convinced myself that I loved her enough to marry her. My cellie, Dennis, thought otherwise.

You fool. You think she ain't out there fucking Sancho for a fix right now?

This was a delusion fostered by being in jail.

She may love you, but she loves that heroin more. I don't need to remind you of this.

Then one day she disappeared.

She's not coming. Quit pacing like an animal.

I can't help it.

Her visits stopped, and she was no longer sleeping at Mom's.

Has your mom heard from her?

Not in three weeks.

The only thing worse than being dumped in jail was hoping that she'd dumped me.

She got that income tax check and ran away with Sancho.

I hope that's it. I hope she ain't dead in a ditch somewhere.

204

When at last we heard from her, she was in jail.

When Mom called the jail they said that Sarah was being charged with five aggravated robberies and a possession of narcotics.

Fuck, Dennis, they also said she's got up to 99 forgeries pending.

She's history. Best you just forget about her.

Buying a car with her income tax check, she had hooked up with two guys, who used her and her car to do robberies.

They were snatching purses from the window of a moving car.

Fucking low-life crime.

She was then writing checks to herself on checkbooks found in the purses, proving that when it came to being junkies, they were rank amateurs.

Sure makes boosting an attractive alternative, don't it?

Sure does. White collar by comparison.

Her brother got in touch with my mom.

If I bond Sarah out, can she stay at your house? She can't leave the state when out on bond, and I live in California.

Sure she can. But you thought Matthew was bad? Now she's really met low life.

But every time she tried to bond out they would just page-two her on a pending forgery charge.

Oh look. You have a new charge. It's back to Madison for booking and a new bond.

Again? I just went through this.

She ended up getting seven years.

Rumor has it they dragged some little old lady across a parking lot.

That's pretty awful.

I never saw her again.

It's lucky they caught her when they did.

Well, you know the old saying: She wasn't arrested, she was rescued.

In the meantime, they were talking about letting me out.

Your pre-sentence report is recommending probation.

My public defender had consolidated all my charges, and we drew Judge Hotham.

I got your new case added on, and, after you plead guilty on it, we'll proceed to sentencing on all three.

He was a decent judge, but I always did have good luck with judges.

And Hotham sees hope for you. I think he likes you.

But I made it clear to my lawyer that I didn't want probation.

That's all very well, but probation is a trick bag, and I don't want nothing to do with it.

The problem was, with all these charges, I couldn't just march into Hotham's court and demand I be sent to prison.

Sentencing on burglary, possession of a narcotic drug, and possession of drug paraphernalia. Have you anything to say?

Yeah. You're weak if you don't give me the max.

Picking up a new charge while out on bond was the same as picking up a new one on probation or parole.

That's your choice. But the judge is being generous here. He feels that you're a good candidate for rehabilitation.

Well, he's wrong.

Under these circumstances, Hotham could've really sent me to prison.

Maybe. But do you really want to tell a judge that? He can give you flat time on all three felonies and run them all consecutive.

I guess you're right.

So I played the contrite junkie...

Yes. I want to be rehabilitated.

...and took intense probation, which is a form of home arrest.

You will have to participate in out-patient therapy for the duration of your probation. Understand?

Yes, Your Honor.

I was also sentenced to six months in jail, with the stipulation that I could be released early into a rehab.

And your time in the county is flat. Day for day. No good time, so I suggest you find a program quick.

My new probation officer, Laurie, wanted me to do a long-term rehab.

I think you need time to lick this addiction. Up to a year in rehab.

That's a long time to do in any program.

But I refused and eventually got accepted into a 28-day rehab in Glendale, a northwestern suburb of Phoenix.

Well, yes, but I think you'd benefit from it. You need structure and discipline that you just can't get in short-term programs.

No way. 28 days is what I was thinking. That, or I finish my six months here.

It was called Maverick House.

Welcome, Mr. Parker. How're you doing.

One day at a time.

God grant me the serenity to accept the things I cannot change; courage to change the things I can; and wisdom to know the difference.

Laurie had taken me there right from jail, and I conned my way through the interview.

Do you feel you're prepared for vigorous rehabilitation, Mr. Parker?

Oh, yes. I've seen the light. Hit rock bottom. I'm powerless over my addiction. I have to give it away to keep it.

I was released to Maverick House a month later and, once I became a resident, I felt I was the one being conned.

I have issues with divine intervention.

I assumed that God, if he existed, would have better things to do than help me with a drug problem.

I knew that roughly 25,000 children died every day on our planet from hunger and preventable diseases.

So to me it was selfish to pray for myself, even if I could believe in God, and especially for something I viewed as utterly insignificant...

...in the grand scheme of things.

My nonfiction friends at Columbia include Bridget and Nell and Glenn and Liza.

And my fiction friends are Dan, Joe, Cesar, and Stephen.

Bridget is in her 60s, a retired producer from HBO, and a New Yorker through and through.

Nell is 28 and from Thomas Jefferson's hometown of Charlottesville...

...while Glenn is the other quintessential New Yorker.

Liza also lived in the city, Pre-Columbia, and is the first in our class to have a book deal.

Although she's nonfiction, her novel is loosely based on her experiences attending high school in Mexico City.

209

Dan, my bar-hopping buddy, was born in Jersey but grew up in Vermont...

...and Joe is also from Jersey.

WELCOME TO West Orange EST 1862

HOME OF THOMAS A. EDISON

Cesar is originally from Medellin and now lives alternately in the city and with his family in Connecticut.

And my friend Stephen is on sabbatical at Columbia from his job as an immigration lawyer in Dublin.

Dan gets me a reading at the Gallery after Liza, who was originally supposed to read, can't make it at the last minute.

Do you want to read at the Gallery?

What? Tonight?

Sure. Why not?

Yes. In about three hours.

He, of course, has to vouch for me to his fellow third-years.

Is this guy a good writer?

Course he is, Trust me

I read a piece I had published as an undergrad.

A common prison cliché about release is "Out the gate at eight, in the spoon by noon..."

It goes over very well.

For my first workshop I have Leslie Sharpe.

She teaches me to trust my voice.

"Just write it the exact same way you would tell it."

It was during her workshop that a fellow student gets on my nerves when I mention John Lennon in an essay.

"He's a cliché for the peace movement."

"Oh? He is?"

I want to smash his face into the table.

"Well, I think you're wrong. I think John Lennon is a cliché for the manifest failure of the peace movement."

For workshop in my second semester I have Michael Scammel, who penned the definitve Solzhenitsyn biography.

Solzhenitsyn
Michael Scammell

I also have Patty O'Toole for my mandatory research seminar.

She's the author of two excellent biographies.

The Five of Hearts
an intimate portrait of
Henry Adams
Patricia O'Toole

When Trumpets Call
Theodore Roosevelt
after the White House
Patricia O'Toole

In addition, I take seminars with nonfiction author Amy Benson and poet Timothy Donnelly.

And a lecture from literary critic Richard Locke.

In her research seminar in the spring of 2008, Patty assigns us Janet Malcolm's "The Journalist and the Murderer."

> It's a thin book, and an interesting read, pushing the boundaries of research.

THE JOURNALIST AND THE MURDERER

As I read it I realize that I was on the same yard as the murderer, and I spring it on the class.

> I did time with Jeffery MacDonald at FCI Phoenix. I've seen him on the yard.

> He kept to himself a lot and wasn't popular. The general consensus was that he was guilty.

> Really? What was he like?

And Bridget knew him, too.

> Oh my God. That's so weird, because I once interviewed him for "The Dick Cavett Show."

The class gets a real kick out of this, Patty not the least.

> Small world, eh?

> And a smaller penal system. Andrew Daulton Lee, better known as the Snowman, was also at FCI Phoenix.

In late April, Richard Locke reveals to us students in his fiction lecture that he has prostate cancer.

> We won't miss any classes. I'll go in for the operation and be back in two weeks, meaning we'll have to extend our semester well into the month of May.

Like I sometimes did for friends in prison, I buy a "Get Well Soon" card and walk around campus getting people to sign it.

> Sign this card for Professor Locke or I'll break your fucking fingers.

> Sure.

> No problem.

> Lend me a pen.

412

413

Two weeks later he's back, in obvious pain as he lectures from a chair.

> I want to first express how touched I was by all the cards and flowers and the endless emails and can only add that the sentiments expressed are entirely mutual.

I graduated from Maverick House in June of 1991.

Oh, you're going to make it, Matthew.

One day at a time.

But I'd already convinced myself that intense probation was geared toward failure for anyone this side of sainthood.

Maricopa County Intense Probation Rules to Live By
No working off the books.
All paychecks to be turned over to the department, which will then decide on redistribution.
UAs and/or breathalyzers will occur randomly three times per week.
You must attend 90 AA/NA meetings in 90 days.

And, I told myself constantly, I didn't want to be a saint.

These rules weren't made to be broken. They were made for fascists.

I couldn't conceive of a world without heroin. I loved it that much.

Sing a song of sixth-sense, a pocket full of high, four and twenty junkies thrown in a sty. When the sty was opened we all began to sing, let's give a cheer for the Heroin king.

So I violated on purpose just a few weeks out of Maverick House and was booked into Madison.

Hi, Laurie. You need to put out a warrant for my arrest.

I already did. For breaking home arrest. Turn yourself in at any police station.

My PO, Laurie, just didn't get that I was happy being a junkie.

Why don't you want to get help with your addiction?

That anyone can be happy being a junkie.

Maybe I'm content the way I am.

And that's just psychobabble.

Please don't. It's my life, and prison is just a part of it.

But that's just denial.

Well, I tried. I'm not gonna lose any sleep over it. Or you.

My biggest hope was drawing a judge that would run my three numbers— the burglary, the possession, and the paraphernalia— concurrent.

Maricopa County Superior Court Judgment of Judges
(The below chart is not a scientific calculation but rather is based solely on inmate rumor.)

Aceto	Hanging
Anderson	Hanging
Gottsfield	Decent
Hotham	Decent
Ishikawa	Hanging
Martin	So-so

I got lucky with pro tem Lindsay Ellis.

This is sentencing for Matthew Joseph Parker on probation revocation.

Lindsay Ellis was a commissioner serving as a judge temporarily.

Have you anything to say, Mr. Parker?

No.

And she was cute.

I see you're a heroin addict.

Yes, Your Honor.

And seemed to know an awful lot about heroin addiction.

Well, statistically speaking, most junkies don't reach a breaking point until the age of 40.

I never forgot this.

At which time they either get clean or go all the way.

Probably because I had a lot of respect for judges in general, and the law in particular.

You've got a good eight years left.

Yes, ma'am.

Or at least the vast area of the law that didn't concern me.

I'm going to take some of those years now.

She sentenced me to 2 years on the burglary, 2 years on the possession, and 1.875 years on the paraphernalia...

IN THE SUPERIOR COURT
OF ARIZONA IN AND FOR
THE COUNTY OF
MARICOPA

PRE-SENTENCE
INVESTIGATION
for

Matthew Joseph Parker
CR1990-011444
CR1990-012803
CR1991-000916

... then made me wait a seeming eternity before saying:

All charges to run concurrent.

I was sent to a tiny, minimum security prison in Safford, where I lived in a quonset hut.

There were four of them making up my dorm.

The area between each hut was fenced off.

A tree grew in that no-man's land just outside my window.

In that tree there sometimes sat a peregrine falcon.

My falcon didn't live there but came and went as he pleased.

At first I wanted to tell everyone, show him off, but I decided against it. This was for me and me alone.

Let's catch it.

Let's kill it.

Let's feed it a candy bar.

Sometimes he would look at me; eye me with a black orb. Then he'd ignore me and start preening.

215

I wasn't thrilled when I learned that the Arizona State Prison system forbids beards on inmates.

I had to shave every day.

Sorry, Parker. You need to go home and shave before I can let you eat.

Naturally, I rebelled.

Fuck this. I ain't shaving no more.

Aren't you overreacting?

This was symptomatic of my personality.

Maybe. But if you try to make me do something, I'll do the exact opposite.

That's a real shock.

In the feds, beards weren't an issue. There were just too many Muslims doing time, even back then.

In ADOC, the only way to get out of having to shave every day was for religious or medical reasons.

Arizona State Prison Complex - Douglas Graham Unit
Grooming Policy
Beards are strictly forbidden due to security concerns, i.e., a radical change of appearance can facilitate an escape. Mustaches are allowed but must not exceed the corner

I tried to get one but was denied.

It looks like you just rubbed salt on your face and neck.

So I decided to use their rote bureaucracy against them.

What will you do now?

Beat them at their own game.

A medical waiver was issued to prisoners on a pink carbon copy.

Arizona Department of Corrections Medical Form

Inmate Shaving Waiver
This medical waiver is issued to inmate_____,
ADOC #_____, for the following reason(s): _____
_____

Staff_____ Inmate_____

White copy, medical;   Yellow copy, admin;   Pink copy: inmate

216

So I grew a beard and carried a pink piece of paper with me at all times.

And what if they open it?

I'm busted.

They checked for shaving waivers at the chow hall and when we went out the gate to work.

My job was building a new medium security prison, Tonto Unit, which sat a few hundred yards from Graham.

After you get this framed out, take your crew over to medical and start hanging drywall.

When asked to produce my waiver, I simply whipped out the folded-up, blank piece of paper.

You got a shaving waiver?

I even rubbed some dirt on it to make it look well-worn

Right here.

It worked beautifully, as they never bothered to open it.

Ok. Go ahead.

Then some guy flooded the yard with blank waivers.

I got blank shaving waivers for sale.

These are no good because the cops know that they were stolen.

On the following Monday, when they asked me to produce my shaving waiver, they opened it up.

Where's your shaving waiver, Parker?

Hey. This is just a blank piece of paper.

They were furious.

This is what you've been showing us? For months?

Yep. I don't like to shave.

And showed it.

You little fucking bastard. Go scrape that shit off your face.

Then come back up here. You're getting a major write-up.

Okie dokie.

I thought for sure that I'd not only lose my job...

Hey. Wait a minute. Hold up, Parker. We can't write him up.

Why the fuck not?

...but maybe do some hole time to boot.

He's been walking around with that beard for months.

So? You fool. We'll look like idiots for letting him con us for so long.

So?

Bullshit. This is the same as forgery, and I'm writing him up for it.

But logic dictated otherwise.

Oh, Ok. So you're gonna go to the sergeant and tell him that, for a number of months, an inmate has been fooling us with a blank piece of paper? And that we never checked it?

I guess you're right. Fuck.

They stood, thinking hard for a long moment, before reaching a unanimous decision.

GO HOME AND SHAVE!

Yes, sirs.

A few months later, on the morning of April 2, I was released, just three days shy of my 32nd birthday.

APRIL 1992

Su	Mo	Tu	We	Th	Fr	Sa
			1	2	3	4
5	6	7	8	9	10	11
12	13	14	15	16	17	18
19	20	21	22	23	24	25
26	27	28	29	30		

With all my possessions in a clear plastic trash bag, they took me cuffed to the bus station.

Handcuffs? Are you kidding me? I'm being released.

Regulations. You're still in our custody.

The guards removed my handcuffs and gave me 50 dollars, 32 of which I spent on my bus ticket.

One-way to Phoenix.

I had 18 dollars left, just enough, I was thinking, for a single fix.

The COs waited with me until the bus arrived. Their job was to make sure I got on the bus.

Do you guys have to be right here?

Well, you ain't got to worry about that with me. I'm a junkie.

Yep. One time we dropped a guy off and, rather than buy a ticket, he went and got drunk instead, caused a scene and got arrested.

Yeah, well, we'll just hang out anyway, if you don't mind.

My plan was to get off the bus in central Phoenix, take a city bus to a dope house, cop some heroin and maybe some coke to go with it, then take another bus to Mom's and get high.

But I changed my mind. For the first time in my life, I decided to play it cool.

I'll go home first and call my parole officer in the morning. Piss clean if he wants me to.

219

On the following morning I checked in.

Hello. Can I talk to my Parole officer, Please?

He's out of town. Call back Monday.

After borrowing a few bucks from Mom, I took 20 dollars down to the I-17 and Buckeye Road, to a trailer park that was known for selling drugs.

I got busted, again, trying to cop from an undercover.

You're under arrest. You have the right to remain silent...

But I did'nt do anything.

I was charged with attempted possession of a narcotic drug and booked into Madison by noon.

I'm setting your bond at $1,100, but you have a Parole hold, so you're not going anywhere.

I signed a plea for the new charge to run concurrent with the two two-year sentences I hadn't even finished yet, but the Judge refused it. I then withdrew my plea, was assigned a new Judge, and the whole, months-long Process started over again.

This new Judge is not likely to do anything different.

Fuck 'em. Let's run it by him anyway. I got nothing but time.

This Judge had the same attitude and gave me 2.5 years on the new charge, stacked—that is, run consecutively with the few months I had left to serve on the burglary/possession.

The time on this new charge won't begin until you've served every day of your original sentences.

May of 2008 ends my first year at Columbia, and I fly home to put a new roof on Mom's house.

As soon as we tear the old shingles off, it begins to rain.

We haven't had this much rain in May in 50 years...

And doesn't stop for three days.

Fuuuuuuck!

I cover the roof in tar paper and plastic, but we still have leaks everywhere.

Bring me another pan.

When it finally stops raining, I finish the roof and fix the water damage throughout the house.

I need to scrape the acoustic off the ceiling, re-coat and texture it, spray it down with kilz, then paint it.

I then have time to visit friends and ride my Harley.

Upon my return to New York, five grand mysteriously appears in my student account. I don't ask any questions when it's direct deposited in my bank, and I use it to pay back rent.

Current Account Balance	$5,000

Would you like to have this directly deposited into your account?

12/13/2007 Tuition Arts	$19,406
12/13/2007 Writing Division Course Fee	$120
01/16/2008 Fed Grad Plus Loan	$15,035
01/16/2008 Fed Unsub Stafford	$6,000
01/16/2008 Federal Stafford	$4,250
01/19/2008 Federal Perkins Loan	$2,500
02/27/2008 Fed Grad Plus Loan	$3,807
06/06/2008 Writing General Scholarship	$5,000

I then fly to Cali for my July visit with Nataly.

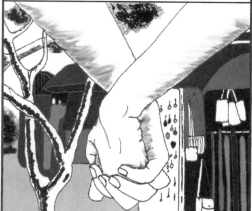

That same summer, after I return from Colombia, Stephen and I go to see Meshell Ndegeocello at BAM.

And I go alone to see Richie Havens at the same venue a few weeks later.

In August, Stephen and I go up to see Zappa Plays Zappa in Peekskill.

In September, Joe and I catch Lou Reed at some club down in the Village.

El Pez Rojo
NO REFUNDS

Reed plays with saxophonist John Zorn, and it's the god-awfullest, most discordant crap you'll ever hear in your life.

BOING!

DWEEB!

TWANG!

It's like having red-hot ice picks driven slowly into each ear.

Maybe Reed is trying to capture something cutting edge from his youth...

This is so hip and so nouveau tech.

So avant-garde.

TWEEP!

...but to us it's the bleating of pretentious dweebs.

MEN

We don't just leave halfway through the concert but are actually driven out.

What is that blessed sound?

New York city traffic.

The following semester I get Patty for thesis workshop.

Fall 2008 - School of the Arts
Parker, Matthew Joseph - mjp2139

57280 WRIT R8023-001
Nonfiction Thesis Workshop
O'Toole, 9.00 credits

80998 WRIT R6225-001
Literary Biography
Scammell, 3.00 credits

58399 WRIT R6215-001
Latin American Lit for the 21st Century
Manrique, 3.00 credits

When I learned this last May, I was upset because, like every other nonfiction writer in Columbia's MFA Program, I wanted Locke.

Did you get Richard Locke for thesis workshop?

No. I got Patty O'Toole.

If you were a DRA you'd have got him.

Don't I know it.

But the admins know what they're doing, and Patty is very good.

So your project is this long memoir?

That's what I've been working on, yes.

I adjust easily, knowing that I'll likely get Locke in the spring.

How goes the thesis workshop, Matty?

Great. I do believe it's gonna work out better this way.

HARLEY DAVIDSON

By this point I'm workshopping 35-40 pages every two weeks.

Chapter 12
Boron
17 pages

Chapter 13
FCI - Phoenix
19 pages

Some of my classmates resent this. Not that I care.

Do you have to turn in so many pages every time?

Yes. But you don't have to read them. Or write a response. I know what you're gonna say anyway.

At 40-plus grand a year just in tuition, I'm determined to milk Columbia's MFA program for all that I can.

There's a party down in Brooklyn on Friday night. Wanna go?

Nope. Gotta stay home and write.

Chapter 12

After getting busted the day after my release from Safford in April of 1992, I was determined to take the new charge, attempted possession, to trial.

There comes a time in a man's life when he just has to nut up. It's time to take a stand against this insane war on drugs.

But my public defender talked me out of it.

You lose a trial, these cocksuckers will give you 12 years. You think they give a fuck about your politics?

So I took the plea and was sentenced to the additional 2.5 years, stacked on the 2 I was already doing.

Where do I sign?

One day in Madison I was in the holding cell of the medical unit for my mandatory physical.

While there I met a Gulf War veteran who'd been shot up pretty bad in Kuwait.

Baghdad
IRAN
IRAQ
Basra
KUWAIT
PERSIAN GULF
SAUDI ARABIA

One bullet had mangled his face...

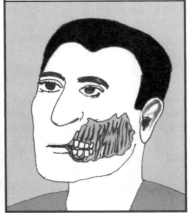

...while another sat lodged still in his brain, atrophying the muscles on his right side.

He moved like he was a thousand years old. He had just turned 20.

After bumming a smoke off me, he told me his story.

I got shot by friendly fire; by my own guys.

You're kidding.

Nope. That happened a lot over there.

He was constantly wiping the drool from his chin with his good arm; drool he couldn't control.

What kind of cop arrests a wounded vet?

After returning to the States, he was arrested for under-age drinking.

They put me on probation that first time.

Yes. Come to Arizona on vacation, leave on probation.

He was then arrested again for the same crime.

I was at a fucking wedding. In a public fucking park when they got me this time.

Because he was on probation, he was being held without bond.

I'm trying to get the army to come get me. Move me to a brig.

Is it better in an army brig?

Fuck yes. This place is unreal. I can't believe they can legally treat people this way.

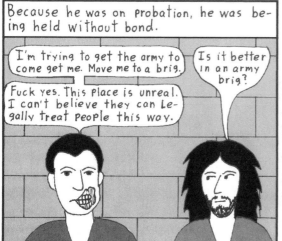

Soon after I was called out, and I never saw him again.

Let's go, Parker.

Good luck to you, man.

Thank you.

225

A few weeks after being sentenced, I was shipped to Alhambra, which is ADOCs way station, like Yuma Unit was in the feds.

Fuck. I was just here a year ago.

Welcome back, baby lifer.

Alhambra was a maximum security prison converted from a psychiatric hospital.

They gave me the exact same battery of tests as last time and classified me as medium security.

I took all these tests already.

Yeah, well, you have to take them all again.

NAME:
ADOC No.
Highest Gr.
Completed:
Sentence:

A month later I was shipped out to Perryville, just west of Phoenix.

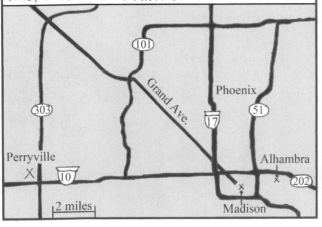

2 miles

It was there, in a medium security Arizona state prison, where I took my first college classes.

Rio Salado Community College	
A Division of Maricopa County Community Colleges	
Course	Credits
HIS 103 U.S. History to 1870	3.00
HUM 101 General Humanities	3.00
BPC 110 Computer Applications	3.00
BPC 111 Micro-keyboarding I	1.00
PSY 270 Personal Adjustment	3.00
SOC 251 Social Problems	3.00
BPC 135AD Wordperfect	2.00
BPC 135AD Adv Micro Key	2.00
LAS 225 Legal Research/Writing	3.00

It was President Bill Clinton who would eventually, in 1994, eliminate the Pell Grant program for prisoners.

The Violent Crime Control and Law Enforcement Act
H.R. 3355, Pub. L 103 - 332

No basic grant shall be awarded under this subpart to any individual who is incarcerated in any federal or state penal institution.

Even though only one-half of 1 percent of all awards went to prisoners.

Percentage of Pell Grants Nationwide 1980 - 1990

99.6%

Percentage of Prisoners Receiving Pell Grants

Thanks, Bill.

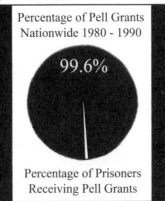

I did not give a Pell Grant to that convict.

In the summer of 1993, I took a legal writing class offered by Rio.

I'm not taking it because of the law. I've had it up to here with the fucking law.

Then why?

It was the word "writing" that attracted me.

Because it concerns writing. I like to write.

Yeah. Writing fucking law.

Our first assignment was to go into the law library and research a case. Any case.

I want you to focus specifically on legalese; words like "whereby," "wherefore," "herewith," "hereto," and "heretofore."

GAL RESEARC ND WRITING LAS 225   RIO SA COMMUN

The next day I randomly pulled a book off the shelf, opened it, again at random...

...and found the appeal of Freddie Thomas, the man who murdered my brother.

COURT OF APPEALS
STATE OF ARIZONA
DIVISION ONE

STATE OF ARIZONA
Appellee

v.

FREDERICK FRANCIS
THOMAS
Appellant

At the time of his death, I wanted none of the details but now there they were, right in front of me.

He had stabbed my brother multiple times and slit his throat.

This served to remind me that violent crime had touched me, too...

...and opened my eyes to the fact that, even if I had come to terms with doing time, I had put myself in the company of monsters.

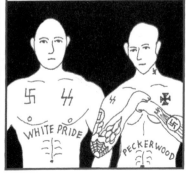

It was in July of 1993 that I went to my first, and last, parole board.

> You're going to your first Parole board?

> Yep. It's my home arrest board.

> You'll never make it.

> You're probably right, but I got nothing to lose.

In the past I simply waived my parole hearings whenever they came up. I didn't have enough time on my first two sentences to make it worth it.

> You're not going to the Parole board?

> Hell no. Even if I made it I'll be out before the board can even act.

Since I still had two years left to serve, I wasn't expecting much when I went before the board that hot July day.

> Hello, Mr. Parker.

And, not expecting much, I told them what I really thought of their rehabilitation policies in general and 12-step programs in particular.

> And why won't you go to AA meetings?

> I just think it's all bullshit.

But I made it.

> I sure hope you're serious.

About three weeks later they strapped a tracking bracelet to my ankle and kicked me out.

> If you leave your house when you're not supposed to, this thing will go off.

> Yes. My electronic leash. When can I go out?

> Once you get a job, you're typically allowed 12 hours out, 12 hours in.

Soon after my release, Arizona passed a Truth in Sentencing Act, which eliminated parole.

Arizona State Senate
Background Brief

The Arizona Legislature passed truth-in-sentencing laws in 1993. Law 1993, Chapter 255, altered earned release mechanisms and abolished parole for offenses commited after January 1, 1994. This legislation also mandated that an inmate serve his or her entire court-imposed sentence, except that a person may be eligible for earned release credits for up to 15 percent reduction of his or her sentence for good behavior.

Mom welcomed me home, like she always did.

Is that comforter on your bed Ok? 'Cause if not, I've got another.

Welcome back.

It's fine, Mom. Everything is great.

Thanks.

The electronic parole officer strapped to my ankle gave her some peace, even if the junk car I had bought didn't.

You gonna be all right driving that piece of shit back and forth to work?

It'll be fine for now, but I still have no license, and that's scary.

She hoped the bracelet would help keep me in line. And for a while it did.

Fuck 'em. Drive without it. I drove without a license for years.

I was chipping, of course, but really didn't get strung out again until a year later, when the thing finally came off my ankle.

You're now officially off home arrest. General parole should be a breeze. Hope you make it, Parker.

I think I'll be fine, thanks.

The whole while I was doing drywall punch-outs on new homes.

What's up with lot 215, Parker?

The usual. There's some plumbing repairs in the master bath, a dozen holes in the lids, and the pot shelves are a fucking mess.

The money was so good that Mom leased me a brand-new truck in her name.

Holy shit.

You won't be getting pulled over in this baby, unless you're speeding or something.

After moving to Scottsdale in 1978, both my mom and my stepfather, Carl, had gone legit.

He works maintenance at a mall and I clean hotel rooms.

Why so surprised? I always had a job, at least before I met Carl.

You both have real jobs? You're kidding?

I know, but you always seemed to supplement a job with larceny.

1978
DECEMBER
3

Carl no longer carried a gun, but Mom still carried a bag of weed.

I could never go that legit.

They both went through the year it took to convict my brother's murderer, never missing a court date or a detail.

I hereby sentence you to 25-years to life.

MCSO

Mom and Carl held it together through John's death, and Mark's death, and then my first tentative steps in and out of prison.

R.I.P.
Harold John Parker
Oct. 9, 1957
Feb. 1, 1980

R.I.P.
Mark William Parker
July 13, 1961
Sept. 28, 1984

It was in the early 90s, while I was at Safford, that they split up.

Carl moved out and we're getting divorced. I guess it's been coming all along.

1991
November
8

My mother needed me now.

You better get your act together. I can't pay this mortgage by myself.

1992
February
5

This was why, when I got busted the day after my release from Safford, it had been so hard on my Mom.

You stupid fuck. I now have to work double shifts just to keep my head afloat.

1992
APRIL
3

By then she was working at a nursing home.

Connie lost her teeth somewhere, and old man Tate pissed his pants again.

Great.

The hotel had fired her, just a month or so before her 10-year pension benefits would've kicked in.

We have to let you go because you were late twice in the last nine years.

You fucking piece of shit MBA.

She worked long hours to make ends meet while I lounged around Madison, waiting to be sentenced.

Man, you've been sleeping for two days.

I've been buying Elavils from the psych cases.

MCSO

This continued through the year I was at Perryville.

July 1992

Su	Mo	Tu	We	Th	Fr	Sa
			1	2	3	4
5	6	7	8	9	10	11
12	13	14	15	16	17	18
19	20	21	22	23	24	25
26	27	28	29	30	31	

August 1993

Su	Mo	Tu	We	Th	Fr	Sa
1	2	3	4	5	6	7
8	9	10	11	12	13	14
15	16	17	18	19	20	21
22	23	24	25	26	27	28
29	30	31				

Now, with my job in construction, I was making much more money than she.

Why don't you pay off your fines and get your driver's license back?

Can't afford it.

Although arrested a few times for driving on a revoked license, I avoided picking up any new felonies.

Bullshit. Stop spending your money on dope.

I'll try.

For the first time in years, she could take a deep breath.

Don't try. Do it. Why do you feel the need to get high every fucking day?

But her respite didn't last long.

Why do you?

231

The Presidential election of 2008 is a whole new scenario.

A lot of things are going to change this year, mate.

Yeah. We'll finally be rid of that fucking Bush.

For one thing, I can vote in New York.

To register to vote in the city of New York, you must:
Be a citizen of the United States (includes those persons born in Puerto Rico, Guam, and the U.S. Virgin Islands).
Be a New York City resident for at least 30 days.
Be 18 years of age before the next election.
Not be serving a jail sentence or be on parole for a felony conviction.

For another, a black man is in the race.

The New York Crimes
Wednesday, January 23, 2008

Obama Gives Speech Defending Roe v. Wade

Otas quam aliquid mo enuecio doluptam, coreptius estotae pudaecae nonsed qui opta nos endi od quo voluptatio ipsam hilique et, cus eaque

videliquis doluptati ut prature mporem consequ identiis aut earume sundem dolorestur? Quis adit est laut eos et que coressintur aut es pa eatius

Mint. Ximus es vid et prernat reprem qui omninod ipectesto doluptatur sitatem quod modiorepel eos maximus aut et liquunt, omnitasi nonet voluptatur si

qui ommodis cidigentis maxim fugitatrem et et abo. Am que dem que sinvell entiameniet que dis accepuditatem adi dolente mporest offic to quas

Polls Put Obama Ahead of Clinton for First Time

Im sum? Hic em Orehenimusaut periatur, non exped ulla nonsequia doluptaquis et laboresse vent

modisinum fugitatis este audue eicipuspedis quiatiis nonved moluptici re, ommodine

Tu temquas explique nulpa ni susdae volorib eatumet quat acerum, sam, sam autfatiis aut rerios

consende quo que quae. Vit reperep ellaut modignis eatur? Qui cone nientis as sed ut et laut

Barack Obama is the coolest mother fucker to ever strut his way onto the American political stage.

Voting for him on the old lever machines is an indescribable feeling.

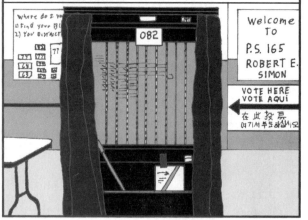

Where do I vo...
1) Find your B...
2) You Distruct...

77

082

Welcome TO P.S. 165 ROBERT E. SIMON

VOTE HERE
VOTE AQUÍ
在此投票
여기서 투표하십시오

Not only is it the first time I can legally vote in 15 years, but pulling that lever felt like a blow to scared white men nationwide.

Take that, neocons.

THWUNK

When Obama wins the election so decisively, I can only snicker over how it's sitting with all those white supremacists dominating American prisons. But I'm glad I'm not there.

We need to put a beat-down on some white boy celebrating that toad becoming President.

Did it right out in the open, he did.

Let's go.

232

There's a festive atmosphere in New York following Obama's election. My friend Stephen, being Irish, is no less caught up in the mood.

Well, mate, yours is the first white nation to elect a black president. Who'd have thought you'd be the first?

Having been an immigration lawyer in Europe, his liberalism at least matches my own, to a point.

I've seen too much suffering; people tortured and women serial raped...

But Stephen, on a student visa, needs a job even more than I do.

...so I try not to complain about it too much, but for fuck's sake, I just need a job.

Only allowed to work part-time on campus, he is snubbed by all the same Columbia employers that have snubbed me.

So why not just work off the books?

And all the same interview committees, which only serves to remind us of the level of cronyism going on at Columbia.

Can't do it, mate, even if I wanted to. I'm a lawyer, after all.

Getting a job here seems to be based more on who you know rather than any real life experience.

It's just not in me. And even if it was, I'd fuck myself good if I got caught.

As an international student, Stephen has to cover most of the expenses related to living in New York out of his own pocket

So you go on, barely surviving. I don't know how you do it.

As a comparison, I have to borrow about 60 grand a year.

Don't have much of a choice, really.

And even that's not enough, which leads me into thinking about fraud.

Well, I do. In case you haven't noticed, I've a bit of larceny in my blood.

Joe is the silent, writerly type and, like Stephen, is in his late thirties.

Hey, Joe...

I'm busy.

He's from Jersey, or, as I like to pronounce it to him, Joyzeee.

He's half Hungarian and half Italian.

Oh, come on. The Yankees are on.

Maybe I'll stop by later.

This makes him, in my eyes, a full-blooded gypsy.

Hey, Joe...

What!

He also seems to harbor an addiction to Hungarian pastries.

...where you going with that pastry in your hand?

Which are served in abundance at the Hungarian Pastry Shop.

Being plagued with roommates, and always, gypsy-like, in the midst of moving, Joe does most of his writing at the Hungarian Pastry Shop.

Look, I know you need a pastry fix, but let's go watch the Yankees instead.

Can't. It didn't go well in workshop today. I'm rewriting my whole book.

A prolific writer, Joe puts too much stock in the criticisms elicited by the obligatory workshop lops.

Hey, Joe, I heard they shot your novel down, shot it down to the ground...

Very funny.

By this time, my friend Dan had moved to Iowa.

"Dan has moved out of New York?"

"Yep, he's gone."

His girlfriend is studying at Iowa's Writers' Workshop.

About six months earlier, Dan had quit drinking.

"Have a beer with me, brother."

"No. What the hell's the matter with you?"

Completely.

"You, of all people, should know better."

"You're right. I'm sorry."

I'm very proud of him, but I miss him something awful.

"Hey, Dan? What's a corn fritter? I've always wanted to know."

"Fuck you, dick head."

Growing up in Vermont, Dan loved the short stories of Charles D'Ambrosio.

We both, along with Billy and Stephen, are Roberto Bolaño enthusiasts.

"Have you seen the size of "2666"? Who's got time to read it?"

"Dan."

It was Billy who had turned me on to "The Savage Detectives" back in 2006.

"You have got to read this guy."

Now he's a big hit around Columbia.

The New York Times

SUNDAY BOOK REVIEW

The Sound and the Führer
by STACEY D'ERASMO
February 24, 2008

Among the many acid pleasures of the work of Roberto Bolaño, who died at 50 in 2003, is his idea that culture, in particular literary culture, is a whore. In the face of political repression, upheaval and

My friend Cesar is from Medellin and lives now in Connecticut.

We need to meet up in Colombia one of these days.

That would be cool.

An accident left him with a spinal injury, and he walks with a cane.

When are you going back?

In January.

Not surprisingly, he's also a big fan of Bolaño.

Do me a favor. Pick up Bolaño's "Nocturo de Chile" for me. I want to read it in Spanish.

Sure.

Cesar holds an annual birthday party for himself, usually in La Pequeña Colombia, better known as the Jackson Heights Section of Queens.

These parties are well attended by, mostly, fiction people.

Although I'd never admit this to a nonfiction person, fiction people are more fun.

Why do you think that is?

Yes. They're always watching and reporting.

I'm not sure. But nonfiction folks are more introverted, not surprisingly, since their writing is more introspective.

I also have a couple of poet friends, but they tend to wander off, as poets are wont to do.

Ain't seen you in some time. Where've you been?

Taking the road less traveled by.

For nonfiction friends, there's Bridget.

Matthew. You look fabulous.

Just got back from Colombia.

Originally from England, she came to New York in the 1960s and never left.

A former TV producer, she worked her way into HBO and was eventually reorganized out.

I did 15 years at HBO, produced the series "OZ," and was given early parole.

CLEAR FIRE LANE FOR EMERGENCY VEHICLES

She bounced around a bit after leaving HBO, then got her undergrad degree in anthropology from Columbia. Her writing got her into the School of the Arts.

I'm fascinated by what I consider dead zones—certain spots in the city where businesses fail, and those areas out in the country with hill people.

Hillbillies, You mean.

Bridget has a beautiful apartment on the Upper West Side, along with a country home Upstate.

She's the New Yorker I call when I need answers.

Where's a good restaurant in the Theater District?

Orsos on 46th street.

She and I go to see the musical "Fela" off Broadway.

We've also seen "The Seagull," on Broadway and catch the occasional opera at the Met.

Try not to get thrown out this time.

I'll do my best.

Nell is in her late 20s.

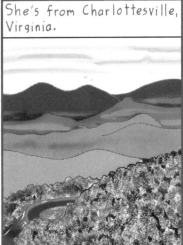

She's from Charlottesville, Virginia.

Nell is very sweet as well as a bit innocent, so we all try to look out for her.

How's your love life?

Ok. I just met this guy and...

Do Not Hold Doors

Do No

I feel the need to screen her boyfriends.

Jack and ginger, please.

You realize if you hurt her I'll break both of your fucking legs.

She's like the daughter of Bridget and me.

How's our Nell?

She broke up with the new guy.

Yeah, well, I saw that coming.

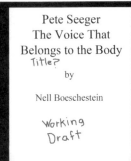

For Patty's Research Seminar, she writes a paper on one of her all-time heroes, Pete Seeger.

Pete Seeger
The Voice That
Belongs to the Body
Title?
by

Nell Boeschestein

Working
Draft

She emails him to plug him for info, and Pete, ever the gentleman, calls her.

Listen to this message, Matthew. It's from Pete Seeger.

Hello, Nell.

Nell ends up working for Seeger, helping him revise his memoir.

You should tell him how much he means to you.

I can't, Matthew. I just can't.

And catches him in concert whenever she can.

Then there's Glenn, a hysterically funny gay Jew.

The last time I looked truly handsome was when I was six.

We are drawn to each other because, like Bridget, Joe, and Stephen, we are closer in age.

It's so nice to have another adult here among all these children.

I agree. Now, let's pretend we're writers.

Glenn went to Roosevelt High in Yonkers, which bussed in minority kids, and ended up sliced into the same sort of compartmentalized racism as prisons.

After gym class one day, a bully threw a rock at Glenn.

Oooof.

Glenn stood up to him, which almost got him killed.

Guess I'll never see that cute boy from homeroom ever again.

But all the girls on the playground came to his rescue, and he was led away in triumph.

Thank you, ladies. Forgive me if I don't partake of your spoils.

This is exactly what you must do if you're ever challenged while doing time.

Um, excuse me, but...

Fuck you, mother fucker.

Prisons, after all, are the ultimate bullies' playgrounds.

In the fall of 1994 I made it off parole for the first and last time in my life. I was strung out again almost immediately.

I need to borrow twenty bucks for lunch tomorrow.

Lunch my ass.

I started getting busted in 1995.

You're under arrest for driving on a suspended license.

Nothing serious, just misdemeanor crap, but it began to pile up.

You have a warrant out for driving on a suspended license. You're also under arrest for driving, again, on a suspended license.

Then I totaled the truck.

Scared to go home and face Mom, I lived on the streets for months.

DANGER
NO
TRESPASSING
VIOLATERS WILL BE PROSECUTED

I rode a bicycle up and down Phoenix and stole cigarettes to support my habit.

Eventually I returned home and, after getting a job, again in drywall, bought a little Volvo station wagon.

JUNKIE
on
BOARD

AZ87078

Picking up two more felonies, I was, amazingly, released on an OR, probably because I had steady employment.

I'm going to release you on your own recognizance.

I failed to appear.

WEST PHOENIX
JUSTICE COURT

TO ANY OFFICER AUTHORIZED
TO SERVE CRIMINAL PROCESS:

Bench warrant issued for
Matthew Joseph Parker
CR95012016 POND
CR9605843 POND
YOU ARE COMMANDED TO
ARREST AND TAKE INTO
CUSTODY THE SUBJECT AND
TO HOLD HIM/HER TO AWAIT

Buying (or copping) heroin was a rush in itself, almost as much fun as shooting it.

I'm going to the Village to cop.

Be careful, baby.

On the East Coast in the 70s and early 80s it was strictly street copping— from black men in the projects.

Whatcha need?

70 bucks.

A New York quarter and two rips.

In order to cop in Bridgeport, I'd walk into neighborhoods that most were scared to drive through.

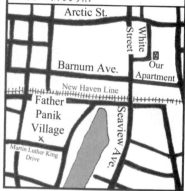

Arctic St.

White Street

Barnum Ave.

Our Apartment

New Haven Line

Father Panik Village

Seaview Ave.

Martin Luther King Drive

The danger there was always in getting robbed.

Give up the dope.

Here you go.

In Arizona, I copped from Mexicans in small housing projects or hotels.

Cuánto, gringo?

A quarter gram of black.

The danger there was getting busted.

You're under arrest for possession of heroin.

But toward the end of the 1990s the Mexicans got smart. I simply beeped them and they'd deliver it right to my front door.

Hola.

20 minutes.

My house.

When I had to fence shoplifted goods, however, I was often left no choice but to go to them in their neighborhoods.

I got 20 packs of cigarettes and 10 bottles of aspirin.

I give you 20 black, no más.

Chapter 13

Cops love junkies.

I brought you something.

I'm not talking about vice cops, or FBI or DEA agents, but just your average city cops who're getting paid very little money to do a very nasty job.

It's beautiful. Can you hold it for me, please?

I hold a lot of respect for these guys.

I had some candy set aside for you but I left it on my other bust.

When dealing with crack heads, PCP addicts, speed freaks, and drunks, their job becomes very difficult, and their lives are often put in danger because all these drug users are unpredictable.

Whaddya got?

Wonderful.

A naked tweeker with a self-modified chainsaw.

253

Delusional, paranoid, desperate, or just plain I-don't-give-a-fuck drunk. Cops hate having to arrest these people.

I was thinking that perhaps you guys wanted to take me in alive, so I built this chainsaw for strictly platonic sexual gratification...

666

Junkies, by contrast, are placid.

Could you step out of the vehicle, please.

Sure.

When arrested I was always nonviolent, and more or less accepting, after the initial shock, of this new turn of events.

Wake up, Parker.

I'm not sleeping. I'm nodding.

Both junkie and cop, therefore, recognize the game being played, and both do their part to play by the rules.

You got warrants out.

I know.

My job was to feed my veins in any way I could, and their job was to try to catch me.

STOP.

BAGARF

Wahooozeee.

The worst I've done during a bust was to give them an alias because I always had warrants out for my arrest.

You got ID?

Nope.

Nothing with your name on it?

No, sir.

What is your name, then?

Mark Parker.

This never worked, but I always got the feeling that cops were amused by it.

It's just one more facet of the game.

Yeah. It breaks up the monotony of all those domestic violence calls.

In May of 1996 I was pulled over in my blue Volvo, ostensibly for a cracked windshield, but really it was because I was driving around trying to cop in a Central Phoenix neighborhood where no white man had any business.

Step out of the car, please.

Yes, sir.

What're you doing down here?

Visiting friends.

The first thing I did was tell them where my syringes were.

Anything on you I should know about?

Needles in my right front pocket.

Cops are more than grateful for this — no one wants to get stuck with a used needle — and these two particular cops were no exception.

Thanks for telling us.

Yeah. We really appreciate that.

We then played the alias game, each making our move as if we were doing nothing more sinister than sitting around a poker table.

What's your Social Security number?

What city were you born in?

When was the last time you were arrested?

And for what?

My bluff was called, and I came up with a flush to their full house, which included my correct name, along with some other, rather incriminating, information.

It looks like you're Matthew Joseph Parker, and that you have 11 warrants out for your arrest.

Seems like you're a popular guy on the local court circuit.

We all laughed about this as they were taking me over to the Seventh Avenue Precinct for fingerprint identification.

Hey, Parker. That might be a new record, you know.

For sure. Eleven warrants? It's certainly a record in my book.

I then threw in my cards, admitting that they won the hand; that I was indeed Matthew Joseph Parker with 11 goddamned warrants out for my arrest.

Ok. You guys got me. But that's the first time I ever failed to appear on a felony.

Is that a fact?

But they said we'd all take a ride to Seventh Avenue anyway, as if we were stopping for a quick beer on a Saturday night before they took me on home.

Hey. You guys gonna charge me with driving on a suspended, giving false information, or paraphernalia?

Naw. What do we look like? A couple of pricks?

This suited me fine. I was in no hurry to get to the Horseshoe.

Take your time, then. And would you mind cracking this back window a bit?

I was given 2.5 years on the new charges.

SUPERIOR COURT OF ARIZONA
MARICOPA COUNTY

JUNE 18, 1996

HON. SILVIA R. ARELLANO

CR 96-05843

STATE OF ARIZONA

v

MATTHEW JOSEPH PARKER

PLEA AGREEMENT

10:05 a.m. State is represented by above.

This time, after another trip through Madison and Alhambra, they classified me as minimum security...

Your risk score is 2.3, Parker. Pretty high.

You're right on the cusp, so don't get any write-ups.

...and shipped me to Winslow.

I'm touring Arizona on the installment plan.

Where I made even fewer friends than usual.

Dude. You want to play some softball?

No.

The yard was crawling with sex offenders.

But minimum security had its perks. After a couple of months I was able to get a job picking up trash along Interstate 40, a job they just don't give to sex offenders.

Once I was trudging up a hill in the snow.

We were just outside Flagstaff, and the scenery was breathtaking.

The sun was out and the effort of trudging uphill through deep snow had warmed me up nicely.

As I crested the hill I spotted two full Michelobs sticking up out of the snow.

Just sitting there, like two perfect brown breasts spilling out of a snow-white bra.

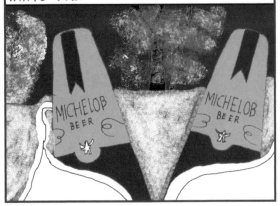

I sat down and drank one slowly while smoking a cigarette, then stashed the other one away for lunch.

This was a perk of the job. All kinds of things were found on America's highways.

Whatcha got?

Looks like speed.

Makeup and women's underwear I smuggled back to the yard and sold to the queens.

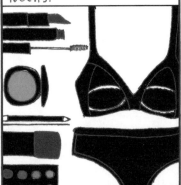

Syringes, sunglasses, pot, drugs, guns, and even bodies were found by the prison highway crews.

I found me a brand-new rig.

How you gonna get it back to the yard?

Underwear and makeup I'd stash in the lining of my jacket. If caught, most cops would've likely let it slide.

Put it in the safe.

The safe? What's the safe?

Up his ass, stupid.

A needle, however, would've cost me my job, my out custody, and got me thrown into the hole to boot.

Ouch ouch ouch ouch ouch!

J John

For my last semester at Columbia, I get Richard Locke for workshop.

That's extrordinary.

And the famous Richard Howard for a lecture.

Kipling spent years wandering the Western Front looking for the body of his son.

And the Pulitzer Prize-winning Margo Jefferson for a seminar.

What did we get out of Zadie Smith's "Dead Man Laughing"?

And finally, from the J-School, Michael Janeway on the critical essay.

Is criticism art?

But although I have fabulous Professors teaching me the art of writing, the bureaucracy of Columbia is another matter altogether.

I can't survive on the money I get from finacial aid.

Hmmm. Have you tried restaurant work?

The only way to get more money out of Columbia is to get my budget increased.

No. But why can't I just borrow more money?

You can. But you must have a legitimate reason to do so.

I didn't bother to mention how hard it is to survive in New York City on 22 grand a year.

Budget		
Bills	month	Year
rent	$1,150	$13,800
cable/phone	$150	$1,800
con ed	$70	$840
credit cards	$200	$2400
Food	$400	$4800
	total:	23,640

Nor did I tell him how productive I've managed to be as a student without my having to work in a restaurant.

I've written 20 chapters since I've been here; 400-plus Pages.

Teacher's Pet.

But I still have larceny in my blood and am not a afraid to use it should the need arise.

I came here to write, not to teach or work like a dog in some damn restaurant for minimum wage.

So I tell them I need $2,300 in expensive computer equipment in order to write a graphic memoir.

Itemized List for Computer Software

DigiPro WP5540 5.5x4" USB Graphics Tablet w/Cordless Pen: $96
GUI Design Studio Pro - User License [#300373767]: $499
Link Electronics HIDE-GRAPHICS drag-and-drop graphics software: $808.50

And another $1,300 for a research trip to Colombia.

Budget Increase Request Form

Airfare...................$500
Hotel......................$700
Car rental..............$100

Department Head

Dean of S of A

Student

And $2,500 more for a new computer.

CRAPPLE 5G
Just $2,499

Made More Cheap in China

These budget increases allow me to borrow that much more money, so technically I'm not stealing anything.

Got another budget increase today.

Man, you've been busy with those, mate.

Gotta survive.

It's a bit more than that, ain't it?

But as soon as I spend the money on something besides what I signed for, I have committed a felony.

Yes. It's fraud.

Are you kidding? Columbia ain't that hip.

Well, if you ever need a lawyer, mate.

I'm in the habit of blaming Columbia for this, but in truth that's just my inner junkie talking. Self-justification is a simple thing, after all.

Hell. They all but encouraged me to do it.

Although it does bother me, because I really am trying to make up for a life of larceny.

Believe it or not, Stephen, as easy as it is to rob them, I don't much like it.

Know what you mean. But bugger 'em, mate. It's all bollixed up anyway. Nobody gives a flying fuck about MFAs.

When I first moved here, I had to assemble all my furniture.

So I bought a lot of tools at a hardware store, along with a $96 piece-of-shit screw gun.

But when I returned home with my new tools, I discovered that the woman at the register forgot to ring up the $96 screw gun.

This can't be right.

So I brought it back the next day and paid for it.

Can I help you?

That's very decent of you to bring it back.

Yes. You forgot to ring me up for this yesterday.

One of the guys working with her insinuated that I was a lop.

You're obviously not from here. A real New Yorker would've never returned it.

Those people were lucky it wasn't the old me in their shop.

Hey. How much for that mason bit behind you?

This one?

No. The half-inch.

249

In the summer I'm offered a job teaching in Columbia's creative writing high school program.

We want you to teach this summer, Matthew.

I know, but you did last year, so if you want the job you're in.

But I didn't even apply for it.

I think about turning it down, since they wouldn't hire me last year, but I need the money.

I don't want this job, Stephen. I feel like somebody, like Patty, threatened them into hiring me.

Fuck it, mate. What do you care? You don't have to kiss anybody's ass for it.

I take the job and find it rewarding, but it's only for three weeks.

The trick is to avoid clichés—to write your poetry or prose in a way that's never been written before.

Poetry
as
Drama
Antigone
v.
the
colonel

Political
clichés
Iron fist
Axis of
Evil

Dan is also teaching in the program and is back in town, from Berkeley this time, where his girlfriend is now working on her Ph.D.

How's your girl?

Even farther.

Far away. How's yours?

I also work for Patty O'Toole as a research assistant.

I'm doing a book of Teddy Roosevelt quotes for Cornell, and I could use some help.

She had an operation on her eyes and, temporarily, can't see very well.

Take these pages to Staples and blow up the font so I can read it.

I'm paid through Columbia's Disabilities Services, but am suspicious about the sheer ease with which I'm hired.

Don't I need to fill out an application or something?

Oh, no. Just have Patty sign your time sheets.

This job, too, was also temporary, as was a short gig I did as a researcher for a well-known sports writer.

I'm doing a book on Joe DiMaggio's 56-game hitting streak.

In the fall of 2009, I get a new job on campus; alcohol proctoring with another fiction friend, Paul.

> Think they'll ask me about felony convictions, Paul?

> Fuck no. Not in a million years. They could give a fuck.

My job is to check IDs at campus events that serve alcohol and to police the crowds for underage drinkers.

> You can't pass your beer to someone else.

> I can't? Oh, I'm sorry. I didn't know. Tee hee.

Police the crowds, just like I police Ivy League law students taking their finals.

> If you have a Mac you must sit in the first three rows. And one seat between each student, please.

I've come full circle.

> Yes, sir, Officer Proctor, sir.

Paul is a Guatemalan from So Cal, and an ex smuggler from Berkeley.

> What were you smuggling?

> Sweet.

> Hashish from Amsterdam. Courtesy of the U.S. mail.

Paul is the first person at Columbia I've met with real traces of larceny in his blood.

> Can't we rob a bank or something? I'm tired of being broke.

> There's no money in banks, and they give you 15 years for that shit.

Which often translates into simple hustle.

> Guess I'll just have to keep working three fucking jobs to survive at Columbia.

He's my boss, more or less.

> Or, like me, you can engage in a bit of freelance fraud.

In November, as I report to the law school to prepare for upcoming finals, Columbia decides to do a background check on me.

Hi, Matthew. Welcome back. I'm from Human Resources, and I need you to fill out some paperwork.

What kind of paperwork?

Just standard stuff. Nothing important.

The space provided on applications for the listing of felony convictions is never big enough.

Have you ever been convicted of a crime? ☒ Yes   ☐ No

If yes, please give the date and describe the nature and circumstances of the crime.

Signature

I have read and understand the above referenced terms and conditions regarding my casual employment at Columbia University

---

At least, not for my convictions.

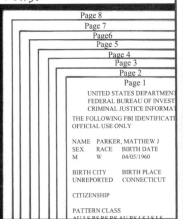

Page 8
Page 7
Page 6
Page 5
Page 4
Page 3
Page 2
Page 1

UNITED STATES DEPARTMENT
FEDERAL BUREAU OF INVEST
CRIMINAL JUSTICE INFORMA
THE FOLLOWING FBI IDENTIFICATI
OFFICIAL USE ONLY

NAME   PARKER, MATTHEW J
SEX   RACE   BIRTH DATE
M   W   04/05/1960

BIRTH CITY   BIRTH PLACE
UNREPORTED   CONNECTICUT

CITIZENSHIP

PATTERN CLASS
AU I S PS PS PS AU PS I S I S I S

In December, just as the exams get into full swing, I receive a letter from Columbia's Human Resources Department.

Columbia University
in the City of New York

Human Resources

Final Notice of Adverse Action

12/23/2009
Matthew Parker
~~█████████████~~
New York, NY 10025

This letter states that, because of my convictions, I'm being fired from all my jobs at Columbia.

Dear Matthew Parker,

We wish to advise you that we cannot give you any further consideration for employment at this time. This action was influenced in part by information contained in a consumer report provided by:
~~████████████~~
~~████████████~~

This includes my law school proctor job, my alcohol proctor job, and any seasonal work like the high school summer program.

But why now? Why wait two years to do a background check on you?

Beats the fuck out of me.

ALFRED LERNER HALL

After complaining to my professors and certain friendly administrators, I'm hired back in the winter of 2010.

I'm sorry about this, Matthew. I don't know what's wrong with those Human Resources people.

Knowing the right people is the ultimate hustle.

Columbia University
in the City of New York

Human Resources

10/25/2010
Matthew Parker

Dear Matthew Parker,

Your case number has been closed. You may now resume your former employment at

---

I've been going to Colombia now three times a year for three years.

So when are you going back to Cali?

Right after the holidays.

My mom is fine with it, although snarky on occasion.

Can't you get laid in Brooklyn?

Fuck a hipster? Not my first choice.

What's a hipster?

It's a... Never mind.

Nataly, typically, can't get a visa to visit me here.

¿Por qué no puedo visitarte en Nuevo York?

Because you are not just Colombian but a poor Colombian to boot.

She was even denied a visa to Mexico.

Embajada de México EN Colombia

Dirección:
Calle 113 No. 7-21,
Edificio Teleport Business
Park, Oficina 204, Bogotá,
Colombia.

Deseo de turismo a México y he sido invitado por una persona que radica allí.

NEGADO

The only way she'll ever see the States is if and when we wed.

When will you marry me?

Soon, mi amor, soon.

We're not quite ready for that.

Not soon enough.

Paciencia, Mateo, paciencia.

She, like me, is a full-time student, studying business and finance.

I need to finish my studies. And so do you.

And, like my mom, a natural-born feminist.

Yo sé.

Es muy importante a mi. ¿Tu sabes?

Nataly knows that financial independence can be the beginning of equality for women in Colombia.

Of course, mi amor.

I need a measure of control over my future.

253

I financed my trips to Colombia with plastic.

PJ Gorgon Chaste

199 72 2008

POUND OF FLESH BANK

Bank of Very Expensive Arts

87 0 78

Upon my release from prison in 2002, establishing credit was a simple thing, despite my criminal record...

I got my first credit card. Ever.

Lucky you.

...and bingeing on it was even simpler.

I'm going to Colombia.

A couple months ago.

Didn't you just get back?

I'm a junkie again, only this time I'm strung out on Nataly.

Necesito tus besos.

Ahora.

Lo sé.

My craving for intimacy is at least as strong as was my craving for heroin.

Thursday, July 23, 2008
Depart: 10:40am, New York, NY
Laguardia (LGA)
Arrive: 7:15pm, Cali, Colombia
Alfonso B. Aragon (CLO)

Thursday, July 10, 2008
Depart: 7:25am, Cali, Colombia
Alfonso B. Aragon (CLO)
Arrive: 9:19pm, New York, NY
Laguardia (LGA)

Total flight cost: $562.70 USD
Please put in your credit card number now:

It's a healthier addiction, aside from putting me in debt, which is a sort of prison in itself.

How the fuck can you afford to be going to Colombia again?

I can't. But I'm going anyway.

Credit is my new heroin, and debt its walls and razor wire.

Federal Correctional Institution Bank 19972

Gank Bank
54 89 04

But after the financial collapse of 2008, the banks start raising the interest rates on my credit cards.

Dear Matthew Parker,

This letter is to inform you that we are raising the interest rates on two of your three credit cards to 25 percent. There's no particular reason for this; you've always paid on time, but we've our own addictions to feed.

Sincerely,
The Bankers
P.S. Thanks for the bailout.

I opt out and/or cancel my credit cards as fast as I can.

I'd like to cancel my credit card.

Fuck off.

We'd like you to reconsider.

In July of 2009, I'm in Colombia for my summer visit with Nataly.

When I check out of my hotel, I learn that my bank has lowered the credit limit on the last card I had money on.

This credit card has been denied.

How could that be? Try it again.

I can't pay my $900 hotel bill.

Hello, bank? My credit card won't work.

We know. We lowered your limit.

I call my sister, Denise, in Arizona and, after much wrangling over the phone with the concierge, we get my bill paid.

I need you to fax me a copy of your credit card.

Can't I just read you it over the phone?

No.

But by the time I get to the airport, I've missed my flight, and it costs me $250 to secure a seat on a flight out the following day.

This only fires my resolve, once I get back to New York, to escape from debtors' prison.

I gotta get out of here.

And how will you do that?

I cancel even more credit cards and, after a slight case of withdrawal and some painful choices, I'm free of immediate debt.

Easy. I'll pay off my credit cards with my student loan money, then not pay rent for a couple of months until I get caught up.

Yeah. Columbia sure is relaxed over you lads being late with rent.

I can only carry honor among thieves so far.

What's with you fucking bankers anyway?

I've an Oxycontin habit to support.

I visit her again in January of 2010.

Sometimes we talk politics.

To Nataly, Barack Obama is just another gringo.

For her, the distinction is strictly geographical.

I happen to be an exception in her encompassing dislike of gringos.

She teases me some more, but I'm trying to be serious.

In response, she kisses me with a laugh, but I push her away.

She's moved from geography to economics.

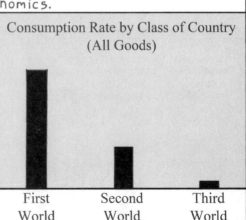

Just as it started warming up in Winslow in the spring of 1997, they shipped me to Yuma.

You're being transferred, Parker.

How come?

What? I'm the fucking warden? How the hell should I know?

They probably think I love it here.

Situated in the extreme southwest corner of the state, it is one of the hottest places in the country.

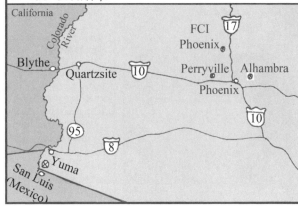

California

Colorado River

Blythe

Quartzsite

FCI Phoenix

Perryville   Alhambra

Phoenix

17

10

10

95

8

Yuma

San Luis (Mexico)

My new job was walking up and down I-10, picking up trash between the towns of Quartzsite and Blythe, California.

My mom drove down for a food visit one weekend, bringing me a steak, baked potato, and corn.

They refused to let her in because she had no sleeves on her shirt.

But I drove here all the way from Phoenix.

Nothing we can do.

They were afraid that my 63-year-old mother, appearing in a sleeveless shirt, would drive sex-starved prisoners into a libidinous frenzy.

Look at those upper arms.

What if I go into Yuma and buy a shirt?

Sorry, you don't have enough time.

I, of course, knew nothing about it and sat on the yard dressed in my prison best, waiting futilely for them to call me for a visit.

Getting a food visit today?

Yep. She should be here any minute.

I was released from Yuma in May of 1998...

Out the gate at eight, in the spoon by noon.

...and violated my parole within a couple of months.

ARIZONA DEPARTMENT OF CORRECTIONS
WARRANT OF ARREST

Current Release Status: TIS
Date of Offense: 5/23/96

TO ANY OFFICER AUTHORIZED TO SERVE CRIMINAL PROCESS
The undersigned has reasonable cause to believe that:

Parker, Matthew   ADC#87078, has violated the Conditions of Supervision and has lapsed or is probably about to lapse into criminal ways or company. . . as demonstrated by his use of opiates on or about 9/9/98, as indicated in a TASC lab report dated

After serving a few more months, I was released, free and clear.

You're back on a parole violation?

There really is no parole. I violated my early release conditions.

I got a job, again in drywall, bought a beat-up truck, and was soon strung out. Again.

It wasn't long before I was boosting cigarettes and other fenceable items.

How much for those aspirin?

These here?

I even boosted on my lunch break so I could get a fix on my way home.

I might be back late from lunch.

Got an errand to run.

How come? Cool.

My mom was angry most of the time, although there wasn't much she could do about it.

When are you going to get your shit together?

I'm trying, Mom.

But as pissed off as she was, I always had a place to live.

Trying, my ass. And take out the fucking garbage, will ya? I gotta go to work.

She was too kind and I used her.

Here's 20 bucks for lunch.

Thanks, Mom.

Then I started getting popped. I was booked into the Madison Street Jail five times from the summer of 1999 to my last arrest ever in March of 2000. The first was for felony shoplifting, three counts out of Tempe. I was never physically caught stealing; they only had me on film boosting cigarettes. Because of this lack of physical evidence, the charges were dismissed, although they could re-file them at any time.

The second was for traffic warrants. These tended to snowball. It might start with a speeding ticket, which is a civil offense, meaning they can't put you in jail for not paying it, but they will suspend your license, which is a criminal ticket. The next time you get pulled over they can, and often will, put you in jail, although they'll sometimes release you if you set up a payment plan. They really just want their money.

The third was for misdemeanor shoplifting, again in Tempe. After a night in their lockup, I was shipped to Madison and was by that time in full withdrawal. After a few days, Mom bonded me out, and as weeks passed I never paid the traffic tickets, so the next time I got pulled over I had warrants and picked up still another suspended license ticket. I was booked into Madison for the fourth time in eight months.

The reason I was always getting pulled over was because all the Scottsdale cops who worked my mom's neighborhood knew me and knew I had a suspended license. I ended up with 90 days in the county on the shoplifting charge and was able to get time served on two of my three suspended license tickets, but the civil fines remained, so when I was released in February of 2000 the cycle started all over again.

It was on March 30, 2000, when I was pulled over in a girlfriend's car about a block from Mom's house.

Awwww, fuck.

There's that fucking Parker again, driving on a suspended license.

Since I just got out of jail, I figured I was clear of any arrest warrants.

Well, at least I know I'm only going to jail for a suspended license.

FK 999

But they had re-filed the felony charges I'd picked up the previous summer, and I was hauled away to Scottsdale City Jail.

You got three warrants out of Tempe, Parker.

That's impossible. What for?

Felony shoplifting.

Fuck.

The next day they shipped me to Madison, where I again kicked in the Horseshoe.

I was classified as maximum security and moved upstairs.

Dude. Maximum security?

I'm always max in the county. Too many prison priors.

On April 5, my 40th birthday, I was standing at my cell door after lockdown.

10

I was thinking about what pro tem Lindsay Ellis said to me before sentencing some eight years earlier.

Well, statistically speaking, most junkies don't reach a breaking point until the age of 40.

A guard, doing his last walk of the night, stopped and bullshitted with me for a moment.

You're a smart guy, Parker. Why do you keep coming back to this shithole?

I had no answer for him, but after he left I got to thinking.

One of the main reasons I started taking drugs was that they told me I couldn't, or shouldn't.

Smoking pot can cause massive brain damage, kids.

NICOTINE
CAFFEINE
COUGH SYRUP

MARIJUANA
GATEWAY DRUG

ALCOHOL, BARBITURATES, AMPHETAMINES-PCP, LSD MMDA, COCAINE, HEROIN

I abhorred control and thought that being a junkie was very clever and very rebellious and very postmodern and very much outside of their control.

You do realize you're a slave to heroin, don't you?

Like an alcoholic has no problems, you mean?

That's crap. I'm my own man, and if heroin were legal I wouldn't have any problems at all.

Then I looked around me.

I was locked like an animal in a tiny cage.

There weren't many places on the planet that offered less freedom.

VORKUTA GULAG

I was totally, irrevocably, utterly in their control and had been for the past 13 years.

Let's go, Parker.

What? I'm the town fucking crier? You'll find out when you get there.

Where am I going?

And in that cell, I was docile and compliant.

I wasn't active. Wasn't rebelling beyond my own internal ravings.

If my pursuit of happiness happens to be heroin, who the fuck are they to stop me from pursuing it.

My poetry was dismal, my essays didactic.

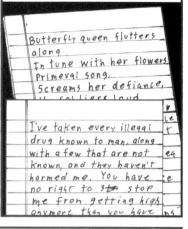

Butterfly queen flutters along
In tune with her flowers
Primeval song.
Screams her defiance,

I've taken every illegal drug known to man, along with a few that are not known, and they haven't harmed me. You have no right to stop stop me from getting high anymore than you have

I had little or no access to education or a forum for my writing where I could get better at it.

Hey, Parker, this is really good.

Yeah. You should publish it.

I wasn't a thorn in the side of The Man, but rather old meat trapped in his intestines.

It was the same twisted logic that I had used to weasel out of voting when I was young.

I'm too cool to vote.

REAGAN BUSH '80

CARTER MONDALE 1980

I had fallen headlong into their snare. I was Arizona State prisoner 87078, a walking fucking palindrome.

They are fucking me coming and going.

I therefore decided, right then and there, to quit using. To turn my life around.

Well, fuck this. I'm gonna quit heroin. I ain't nobody's fool.

It was as simple, and as difficult, as that.

But, man, I sure wish I had me some heroin.

262

In early March of 2010, Bridget and Nell plan a party for my 50th birthday.

You have been invited by Bridget and Nell to Matthew Parker's Big Birthday

BEWARE OF PIRATES
Invitation to Matthew Parker's 50th (Yeah!) Birthday Gathering!!!

The party will take place April 9, in Bridget's apartment, four days after my actual birthday.

Here's something you'll never hear:
"Matthew Parker...he's the one who always wears bow ties, right?"
No, a bow tie would not suit this wonderful man we all know and love.
The real news, however, is that this wonderful man is turning the big 5-0 on Friday, April 9. Let's get together

In each college I've attended, I've always had one female Professor who went out of her way to help me.

At Scottsdale Community College it was Sandra Desjardins.

You have an uncanny ability to draw love to you.

At Arizona State, it was Elizabeth McNeil.

Let's talk about your thesis over dinner, then we'll go see Kneedeep.

And at Columbia, it's Patricia O'Toole.

You did good, kid. You did really good.

Thanks.

Patty volunteers to fly my mom in for my 50th birthday Party, Paying for the airline ticket with frequent flyer miles.

You can't do this, Patty. It's too much. My mom does not need to be here.

Think about it. I bet your mom would really like to be there.

I'm moved beyond words by this and try to Pay back Patty in my own way.

I fly to Colombia the week of Easter and celebrate the holiday, as well as my birthday, with Nataly and her family.

Feliz Semana Santa.

Feliz Semana Santa

Feliz Semana Santa.

Feliz cumpleaños.

I even go to Easter Mass with them.

The following day is Monday, April 5, my actual birthday.

April 2010

Su	Mo	Tu	We	Th	Fr	Sa
				1	2	3
4	⑤	6	7	8	9	10
11	12	13	14	15	16	17
18	19	20	21	22	23	24
25	26	27	28	29	30	

I spend almost the whole day alone in airports, flying back to New York from Colombia.

Alfonso Bonilla Aragón Internat..

MIAMI INTERNATIONAL AIRPORT

This seems fitting, as it is the 10-year anniversary of my epiphany in Madison.

I turned 40 today.

Happy fucking birthday.

Now I'm trading temporary confinement in airplanes...

Flight time to Miami is approximately three hours and 30 minutes.

...for the freedom to move thousands of miles in a few hours.

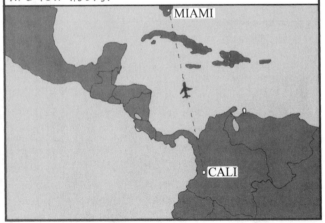

MIAMI

•CALI

My birthday bash at Bridget's is a great success.

You sure know how to throw a party.

Well...

Bridget is a fabulous hostess and cooks a big pot of chili to feed the 40 or so guests...

Who wants salad? And there's a vegetarian dish over here.

...and Nell, knowing it's a favorite of mine, bakes me a carrot cake.

This is delicious, Nellie.

I made it from scratch.

My mother is there with her sister Beth and Beth's son, Mario, along with his wife, Vanessa.

HAPPY BIRTHDAY, MATTHEW!

Richard Locke is also there, and of course Patty and Joe and Paul and many other friends.

Noticeably absent are Dan and Stephen and Billy and Gwen and Alex and Ed...

...as well as, of course, Nataly...

...not to mention Sandy and Elizabeth.

Chapter 14

Alhambra is the ADOC's classification station and is your first stop after being sentenced to prison in the Maricopa County Jail.

Located in East Phoenix, I've been through there four times.

Arizona State Prison Complex - Phoenix

Alhambra Reception Center

2500 E. Van Buren St.
Phoenix, AZ 85008
Arizona Department of Corrections

It's a maximum security yard where your custody level, physical and mental health, and education level will be determined.

Basic reading and writing exam
Basic math exam
IQ test
Basic physical exam
Basic dental exam
Basic psychiatric exam
Security classification
Prison designation

You'll be there from a few days to a few weeks before being shipped out to whatever yard they decide to ship you to.

> Where do you think they'll send me?

> You won't know until you get there.

It's crowded, dirty, and only offers one option for you to pass your time.

> What? There's no books? No cards? No games?

> Nothing but goddamned Bibles.

All other books are banned.

So I wasn't at all surprised that the ADOC administrators at Alhambra wouldn't let me claim my own faith.

> Religion?

> Pagan.

> There's no such thing.

> You better read your history books.

She had a list of ADOC approved religions and mine, a mere generalization, wasn't on it.

> Sorry. It's not on my list. Are you a Wiccan, then?

> No.

After my fourth time through Alhambra I had a pentagram tattooed around my belly button...

Panel 1:
...mostly to piss off my keepers.

Go get Parker in dorm three.

Which one's Parker?

The Satanist.

Oh, yes.

TO SERVE AND PROTECT THE PEOPLE OF ARIZONA BY SECURELY INCARCERATING CONVICTED FELONS...

Panel 2:
I'm neither pagan nor Christian and put the damn thing on there out of sheer spite.

The cops all think you're a Satanist.

It just proves their own ignorance.

Panel 3:
Now it's just a symbol of my own obstinance that I have to justify or explain constantly.

But you have that Pentagram on your belly.

It was originally a symbol of Peace.

Panel 4:
And Nataly hates it.

No me gusta.

Yo también.

Panel 5:
I'd been pulling shit like this since the fourth grade in Catholic school, when I refused to cut my hair.

You need to conform to our grooming policy.

But Jesus had long hair.

Panel 6:
My teacher, Sister Magdalene, would put pink ribbons in my hair and taunt me in front of the class.

Look at the pretty little girl.

HA HA HA   HA HA HA

Panel 7:
Red-faced, I'd always remove them, and she'd always respond with violence.

My teacher hit me again

So why don't you just get a haircut?

No.

Panel 8:
I failed fourth grade that year and was kept back. Much to my relief, my mom moved me to public school the following year.

THOMAS HOOKER SCHOOL

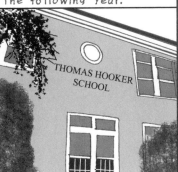

Panel 9:
After that, whenever someone in authority would tell me to do one thing, I'd do the opposite.

You should wear a helmet when you ride, young fella.

No.

Panel 1:
My drug use was a good example...

Drugs will fry your brain.

No, they won't.

Panel 2:
...as were my tattoos.

Panel 3:
I put my first tattoo on my arm when I was 12.

You have to be 18 years old to get a tattoo.

No, I don't.

Panel 4:
I now have 14 tattoos, all but one done illegally in prison.

Why do you have "Jezebel" tattooed on your chest?

Jezebel is symbolic of religious intolerance.

She's what?

Panel 5:
It was something they told me I couldn't do, so I did it.

An illegal tattoo is defined as any means to mark the skin with any mark that is placed by aid or instrument on or under the skin.

Inmate orientation

ADOC-Safford Graham-

Panel 6:
I quit high school in my freshman year because they kept suspending me for smoking on school grounds.

Three-day suspension for smoking. Third one this marking period, Parker.

Big fucking deal.

Panel 7:
Once I missed x number of days, I would automatically fail no matter how good my grades were.

Harding High School Bridgeport, CT	
Grade Report for: Parker, Matthew Joseph	Final Grade
English.....................95	65
Science.....................97	65
Social Studies.............90	65
Art.............................95	65
Metal Shop..................90	65
Blueprint.....................90	65

Panel 8:
It never occurred to me that the suspensions were a result of my own actions...

Why don't you just smoke across the street?

Fuck that.

Panel 9:
...or that sometimes you just gotta play along to get through life.

They should have told you not to go to college when you were young.

That probably would've worked.

In the spring of 2000, I pled guilty to one felony shoplifting in exchange for them dropping the other two.

Did you in fact steal 20 packs of cigarettes from the Short Stop Store in Tempe?

Yes.

The judge gave me 2.5 years in ADOC.

You are also ordered to pay $180 in restitution and a $2,000 fine.

I went through Alhambra for the fourth—and last—time and was again given the same battery of tests.

These fucking tests again?

Yes.

TESTING

What do you care? Would you rather be locked down all day?

I made sure I passed the Psych test, which was given by a tape recorder. Failing the psych test could've led to them force-feeding me psych drugs throughout my stay.

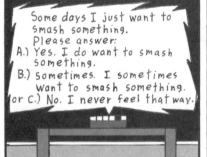

Some days I just want to smash something. Please answer:
A.) Yes. I do want to smash something.
B.) Sometimes. I sometimes want to smash something.
or C.) No. I never feel that way.

I purposefully flunked all the rest—I'd had it up to here with ADOC's idea of education. I even made little designs in the scantrons.

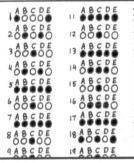

They classified me as medium security and shipped me to a yard called Winchester in Tucson.

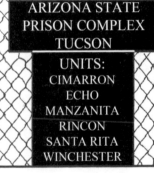

ARIZONA STATE PRISON COMPLEX TUCSON

UNITS:
CIMARRON
ECHO
MANZANITA
RINCON
SANTA RITA
WINCHESTER

Initially, I had to take basic education classes because my test scores were so dismal.

Looking at your scores from Alhambra, Parker, you sure got stupid over the last four years.

That's because I'm sick of playing your prison games.

The administrators at Winchester weren't buying that I had flunked them on purpose.

Yeah, right. It wasn't your drug use that fried your brain.

Heroin doesn't do that. But why the fuck am I arguing with you about it?

I had to have Mom send in my high school diploma to prove that I had one, but this was all just a racket to them.

Parker has a high school diploma. It's on record.

Yeah, well, keep him in school until he proves it.

Prisons get federal money for educating prisoners. It was why the BOP gave me $25 when I got my GED 12 years earlier at Boron.

The feds pay you to get a GED?

Yep. They'll put 25 bucks right on your books.

Winchester Unit at ASPC Tucson was the most corrupt yard I'd ever been on.

Why don't the state do that?

Because they're too fucking cheap.

We were allowed to shop once a week and, when state audits rolled around, tens of thousands of dollars would be hidden on our books...

Hey, there's 60 grand on my books.

50 on mine.

Same here. I only had 30 bucks last week.

COMMISSARY

...and, of course, gone by the following week on store day.

Is all that money gone from your books?

Me, too.

Yeah. Back down to my usual 20-dollar-a-week state pay.

Winchester was also a drug offender yard. Every prisoner there attended rehab classes three hours a day, five days a week, for nine months.

What are some triggers that might get you on a slippery slope toward using again? Anybody? Anybody at all?

With so many drug offenders gathered together on one yard, there was naturally a lot of drugs to go around.

The sack is hitting the yard today.

Heroin or speed?

Both, I think.

Shit.

With all that dope on the yard, it was a challenge to stay clean, but I had made up my mind, slipping up only twice, on Christmas and my birthday.

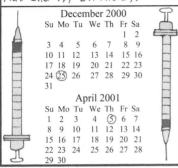

December 2000

Su	Mo	Tu	We	Th	Fr	Sa
					1	2
3	4	5	6	7	8	9
10	11	12	13	14	15	16
17	18	19	20	21	22	23
24	(25)	26	27	28	29	30
31						

April 2001

Su	Mo	Tu	We	Th	Fr	Sa
1	2	3	4	(5)	6	7
8	9	10	11	12	13	14
15	16	17	18	19	20	21
22	23	24	25	26	27	28
29	30					

After a year on Winchester, I was dropped to minimum security and transferred to Manzanita, another medium yard on the Tucson complex.

Why is everything so small?

Manzanita was built for women.

It was there that I met and worked with writer Richard Shelton.

Your poetry is dismal and didactic. Try writing me an expository essay.

And I was at Manzanita when 9/11 happened.

The yard is on lockdown until further notice.

We don't have any guard towers.

Guess they're worried we'll crash an airplane into the guard towers.

You're right. I'll be damned.

A few weeks later, they transferred me to the minimum security Fort Grant, which is out by Safford.

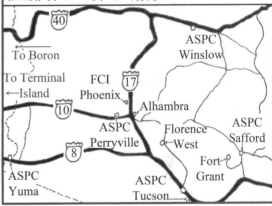

I was able to attend Shelton's workshop only three or four times before they moved me.

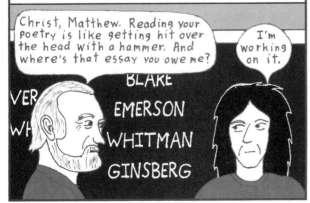

Christ, Matthew. Reading your poetry is like getting hit over the head with a hammer. And where's that essay you owe me?

I'm working on it.

BLAKE EMERSON WHITMAN GINSBERG

But I wasn't sorry to go. Fort Grant, as it turned out, was the only prison I've ever been in that had a view.

271

Around Thanksgiving of 2001, Mom came up to Fort Grant for a food visit, where, after the meal, we filled the time with small talk.

How's Denise? Fine, fine.

And her kids? They're doing good.

She kept a brave face on a grim situation.

And how are they treating you here? Do you like it better than Tucson?

She was strong. She had buried two sons, and the third was in prison.

Oh, yes. I mean, it's still prison, but like most minimum yards, we have a lot more freedom.

The fact that my mom was there at all was a testament of love.

I'm telling you, Mom, that I quit using. I've heard that bullshit before.

By this point she had lost all hope.

But it's true. It may be true now, but what'll happen once you get out?

At 41 years old and on my fifth trip to prison, she saw no reason for hope.

I'd like to go back to school. We've been down this road before, Matt. Talk is cheap.

Over the years I'd convinced her of nothing except my own lust for oblivion.

Well, we'll just have to wait and see, then. Yes, we will. But I'm not putting up with it for long.

My mom much preferred me to be in prison, because she knew I was relatively safe when locked up.

When you're in here I have to struggle to make ends meet, but at least I know I'm not gonna find you dead one day.

So my assurances that drugs were no longer a part of my life were just more empty talk to fill the empty spaces.

You won't. I promise. I'm burned out on it. We'll see.

But my mom never gave up on me — I think because our shared struggles showed her how bad it could get.

I don't have to move back home, you know.

Oh, please. Where're you gonna go?

We were still a family, not despite but because of all that we had lost.

I have other options.

Yeah, like a half-way house. Great choice, since you've done so well in them in the past.

Not that my mother had any faith in my cleaning up.

Well, it's a moot point, since I won't be using no more when I get out.

Oh, brother.

She had come to accept the fact that I was and always would be a junkie.

But, Mom, I'm telling you that...

Matthew, can we please just drop it?

My mom loved me despite this, and drove 300 miles, packing a pistol along with her medicine bag, to bring me a decent meal.

I wish you would'nt come up here with a piece and a bag of weed.

I ain't driving across that desert unarmed and sober.

She knew how to get by.

They have dope sniffing dogs, you know.

What? Was I born yesterday? I stashed it all on the road about two miles out.

I'm tired, mom. So fucking tired.

So am I, sonny boy. So am I.

She was not convinced of my commitment to kick heroin until a year after my release, during my second semester at SCC.

I got straight A's again, Ma, and made the dean's list.

I always knew you had it in you.

I think that was the first time in 40 years that my mom could truly relax.

Whew.

273

I served roughly 11 years in jail and prison...

"I gotta do nine months in this fucking jail."

"Please. I got more time in on the toilet."

...and, thus far, roughly eight years in school.

"They say it can take up to five years to get my MFA."

"If you choose to milk it that long it can."

I owe eight grand in fines to the State of Arizona...

Dear Matthew Parker,
Your outstanding debt to Maricopa County is seriously delinquent. These debts need to be paid in full or there will be serious legal repercussions, up to and including garnishment of wages. Please make check payable to:
Halcyon Days Collection Agency
PO Box 1734
Hawthorne, New Jersey

...and, including ASU, over 200 grand in student loans, and still counting.

Columbia Student Loans 2007 - 2009	
Federal Subsidized	$8,500.00
Federal Unsubsidized	$14,306.05
Federal PLUS	$43,335.10
Federal Subsidized	$8,500.00
Federal Unsubsidized	$13,517.56
Federal PLUS	$39,450.02
Federal Subsidized	$8,500.00
Federal Unsubsidized	$12,688.56
Federal PLUS	$10,202.81
Federal PLUS	$2,789.64
Total	$161,789.74

I refuse to pay the first...

Dear Halcyon Days,

You bought some bad debt from Maricopa County. I did every day on all four of my prison sentences in Arizona. The fines levied against me, therefore, are just an afterthought. They cannot legally fine me and send me to prison. That is double jeopardy. So your efforts to get me to pay these fines are a wasted effort. I won't pay them and you can't make me pay them. So just shove your fucking threats up your sunny-day asses, you lowlife

...and don't think I'll ever be capable of paying the second.

$200,000

Divided by maybe 30 years of life left in me,
= $6,666 per year,

or $550 per month

And that's not even counting the interest.

The difference is that, to me, my student loans are worth every penny.

"Isn't there some way we can avoid paying back our student loans?"

"Probably, but I'm done with larceny."

I view all the time I did in prison as wasted...

"What're you doing today?"

"Getting another tattoo."

...while most of the time I did in school as productive.

"What're you doing today?"

"I've got to finish two more chapters for workshop, then I have to read "Homage to Catalonia.""

It's an easy thing to spend my days looking forward as I traipse through the ivy.

What's your plans for the future?

Don't know. Maybe teach, maybe a Ph.D. Probably both.

But it's in looking back that I gather my strength.

Speak, Memory

Vladimir Nabokov

I'm surprised that I even survived.

Third time's a charm, He was a lucky little devil.

Billy Cioffi and the Monte Carlos

Any fool, however, can simply survive.

I can do this 10 years standing on somebody else's head.

The trick is not just to grow in unexpected ways but to be happy doing it.

Do you have to turn in so many pages for workshop?

Yep. Gotta milk Columbia for all I can get.

Even in Prison I was a happy guy, relatively speaking.

Do you have to be so thrilled Picking up trash?

Yep. I'm outside of that fucking Prison.

And I achieve my happiness by being grateful for what I have.

And things could always be worse. I'm healthy, and I know I'll be going home soon.

Comparing my years in prison to years in the Russian gulags, say, made my time easy to do...

Man, you're crazy. We're doing hard time here.

Oh, bullshit. this is Camp Snoopy, comparatively.

... just as walking in Central Park makes me grateful for my legs.

It's a beautiful thing to be able to walk in the park. Central Park is my favorite...

...but there's also Riverside Park...

...and Inwood Hills Park...

...or indeed any park anywhere.

Parque San Antonio
Santiago de Cali

All serve as reminders of just how lucky I am—how lucky we all are to be living free in a world where the leisure to take such walks is possible.

Wow. It's amazing.

Yes.

Gratitude comes easily to me these days.

I'm returning to New York soon. Are you not sad?

A little.

What I've garnered from this is that you have to work your ass off for everything of any real worth in life.

Only a little?

Yes. Because I know you will return.

It took me in excess of 40 years to learn this lesson...

Oh, really? And you are certain of this?

Por supuesto, mi amor. Of course I am.

...but Nataly knows it instinctively.

Trust is not such a simple thing, but love is empty without it.

While in prison, I yearned for the normal and the mundane.

Look at those lucky mother fuckers out there.

Yep. Just driving home from work.

I think about this a lot.

You're becoming awfully bourgeois, Matthew Parker.

I'm morphing into a productive member of society.

My most blatant act of hedonism these days is late-night cookies and milk.

One sure sign of this is my applying for an American Express Gold Card in April of 2010.

Fines?

Student loans?

An ex con with a no-limit credit card?

Eighty-five hundred.

Plus two-hundred grand.

Priceless.

Although I really only want it to try to get presale tickets for Roger Waters' "The Wall" concert that's coming to Madison Square Garden in October.

ROGER Waters The Wall

Live at Madison Square Garden. October 5, 2010 Presale with American Express Gold Card Only

Surprisingly, I'm approved.

MATTHEW J PARKER CARDMEMBER SINCE YESTERDAY

AMERICAN EXPRESS

I end up paying $277 for one ticket.

ticketslave

Come October I go alone to the concert.

Which is well worth the wait and even the price.

After the show, I blend easily into the crowd.

Some find it odd that a guy who hates crowds could so love crowded New York City, but it's a different sort of crowd here.

1967

New York is anonymously crowded; far from the in-your-face privacy invasion of overcrowded prisons.

ARYAN

88

It's a place where nobody wants to know your name or you DOC number or your race or your criminal history or even your god-damned religion.

Any gang affiliations?

Yeah. Catholic.

ASPC - Phoenix
Alhambra
Reception
Center
Please inform intake officer of any medical or psychological problems immediately

And nobody wants to see your asshole...

ALL INMATE WORKERS MUST BE STRIP SEARCHED DAILY
NO EXCEPTIONS

Now bend over and spread your cheeks.

...except maybe for a few strays cruising the Ramble...

...or a customs agent at Kennedy Airport.

What country are you coming from?

Colombia.

Step into this room, please.

ACKNOWLEDGMENTS

So many people have contributed to the writing of this book that it will be impossible to name them all, but a bevy of standouts are listed below:

Starting earliest at Scottsdale Community College, I owe a debt of gratitude to Sandy Desjardins and Robert Mugford. Thanks also to Eric Loring, Steven Mutz, Mark Klobas, Connie Carruthers, and Ginny Stahl. From my job at MCTV special thanks go out to James and Lorie O'Brien and Mark Grossman and Laura Carruthers.

At Arizona State University, Cynthia Hogue, Heather Hoyt, Amy Lerman, John Lynch, Matthew Whitaker, Paul Morris, and Ayanna Thompson were just a few of the outstanding professors I had. And of course I can never forget Elizabeth McNeil, who guided me expertly through the mounds of bureaucratic bullshit like a seasoned convict holding out on some forgotten rock.

At Columbia, thanks to Amy Benson, Timothy Donnelly, Bob Holman, Richard Howard, Michael Janeway, Richard Locke, Margot Jefferson, Honor Moore, Patty O'Toole, Michael Scammell, and Leslie Sharp. From admin special thanks go out to Dave Beeman, and, from financial aid, I'm grateful to Tarin Almanazar, Diana Parra, and Daniel Rodriguez, all three of whom saved my ass from pauperism more than once.

From Columbia Law, I owe very special thanks to Kristine Chua, who gave me a job when no one else would.

From the Arizona State Prison Complex in Tucson, I owe big thanks to Richard Shelton, poet, writer, and professor emeritus of English from the University of Arizona, whose creative writing program I was lucky enough to attend for a few short weeks.

I'm indebted to my editor, Patrick Mulligan at Gotham Books, who patiently put up with my impatience throughout the process, even when, on occasion, I went all convict on him.

From Kuhn Projects, I owe tons of gratitude to my

agent, David Kuhn, for, among other things, seeing the obvious when I was completely blind to it. To Jessi Cimafonte, who steered me skillfully through that first rough draft, and to Billy Kingsland, who smoothed the way between my publisher and me.

I'm very grateful to my cousin, Mario Recupido, who guided me expertly through my first tentative steps with graphic arts programs.

Finally, in no particular order, thanks to Walt Richardson, Paul Alvarez, Gwen Cioffi, Ed and Michelle Davis, Genevieve Burger-Weiser, Alex Holland, Paul Darrow, Chris Brown, Sunny and Charley Morley, Marlon Burno, Mike Mader, Duane and Reba McClendon, Roberto Taddei, Billy Webb, Mickey McGee, Vince Mancini, TR Hummer, Xavi Forns Rodelas, Ruchika Tomar, Gregg Steinke, Cesar Polonia, Bilal Tanweer, Glenn Michael Gordon, Olivier Zahm, and Murwarid Abdiani.

Special thanks to Bridget Potter, Liza Monroy, Dan Bevacqua, Stephen Collins, and Joe Colonna, all of whom critiqued parts of the first draft and offered advice and encouragement in abundance, and to Nathan Catlin, my intern, who did hundreds of pages of layout work for me.

To Patricia Kim, for company and cigarettes in earnest.

And, with infinite gratitude, to Nell Boeschenstein, country girl and confidant, who read and proofed the entire finished draft, and to Billy Cioffi, for friendship, editing, and live music on the side.